MARKETING
CORPORATE
IMAGE

The Company As Your
Number One Product

James R. Gregory

with

Jack G. Wiechmann

NTC Business Books
a division of *NTC Publishing Group* • Lincolnwood, Illinois USA

Library of Congress Cataloging-in-Publication Data

Gregory, James R.
    Marketing corporate image : the company as your #1 product / by
James R. Gregory with Jack G. Wiechmann.
        p.   cm.
    Includes bibliographical references and index.
    ISBN 0-8442-3282-3
    1. Corporate image.   I. Wiechmann, Jack G.   II. Title.
HD59.2.G74   1991
659.1—dc20   90-26392
                                                      CIP

Published by NTC Business Books, a division of NTC Publishing Group
4255 West Touhy Avenue
Lincolnwood (Chicago), Illinois 60646–1975 U.S.A.
© 1991 by James R. Gregory. All rights reserved.
No part of this book may be reproduced, stored in a retrieval system,
or transmitted in any form or by any means,
electronic, mechanical, photocopying, recording or otherwise,
without the prior permission of NTC Publishing Group.
Manufactured in the United States of America.

1 2 3 4 5 6 7 8 9 BC 9 8 7 6 5 4 3 2 1

Dedicated to my wife and partner,
Evelyn
and our children,
Becky and Bill.

Contents

Foreword

■ It would have been impossible for me not to develop a profound respect for the concept of corporate image. For one thing, my boss and mentor, Fairfax Cone of Foote, Cone & Belding, had written, as a tenet of advertising, "The fact of the matter is, a promise is only as good as its maker."

The accounts I worked on as I learned my craft as a copywriter and creative director had strategies solidly rooted in that notion. For example, Hallmark Cards promised that the recipient of the card you sent would recognize that you cared enough "to send the very best." How could that be when it was chosen from a long line of racks that offered little or no identification of the manufacturer? It had to do with a regular series of television dramas, the Hallmark Hall of Fame, that represented the epitome of artistic quality in that medium. It continued with commercials demonstrating the dedication to fine craftsmanship and good taste that drove the employees of Hallmark. And it ended, as did each commercial, with hands turning over a card to show there was indeed a way to know the sender cared enough: the famous crown logo.

I worked on the S.C. Johnson business. This family-owned company in Racine, Wisconsin, was so dedicated to product research that it chose as its symbol the research tower it had had designed by Frank Lloyd Wright. This corporate image, so vital that it transcended Johnson's identity as a floor and furniture wax manufacturer, made it possible to launch a line of insecticides, Raid, that quickly took over first place in the category.

I worked on Kraft and found the effectiveness of every ad and commercial I wrote for any of its products multiplied by the acceptance of that company's obsession, exhibited on the Kraft Music Hall, with "good food and good food ideas." I worked on Sunkist and discovered that concentrating on the citrus growers who make up this cooperative, talking about their dedication to quality, letting them say about each orange, "Our guarantee is printed on the back of each package," was the key to successful product advertising.

No, I am not dispassionate on the subject of corporate image. In 1970 I gave my first talk to an annual meeting of the American Association of Advertising Agencies. The subject was what I called "The Maker's Mark," the distillation into communications terms of everything that makes a company unique and important to its principal audiences. Expressing this in every message for every one of its products or services, as well as in communications about the company itself, leverages every dollar spent on media. Jim Gregory makes the point far more cogently in the pages that follow.

In 1974 when many companies, particularly those in the energy industries, were being brutalized and misrepresented in the press, it seemed to me time for a new kind of advertising that would state the company's positions without filtering them through an often hostile editorial apparatus. I began giving speeches and writing articles encouraging what I named, revealing a lifelong fondness for alliteration, "advocacy advertising." Jim Gregory provides you with a contemporary look at the subject in Chapter 6.

During my years in Washington as a lobbyist for the advertising agency business, I encountered many critics of advertising in general and of image advertising in particular. Some even took the position that salesmanship and persuasion are essentially unfair and that ads should be limited to price and function information. When I asked if the reputation and aspirations of the people providing the product or service weren't important elements of information, the critics would dismiss that as "hype." My response was generally, "If surgeons could advertise, and you had an inflamed appendix, would you want their ads limited to price and function information?"

So there are still some who are unconvinced about the value of corporate image communications. I hope they will come across this book. And I hope those who have picked it up as a result of an existing recognition of how important the subject is will absorb and profit from the revealing case histories and good, sound counsel with which Jim Gregory has packed these pages.

John E. O'Toole
President
American Association of Advertising Agencies

Preface

■ If you have just picked this book up in a bookstore to see if it's useful, *buy it immediately*.

If you've already bought it and are just settling down to read it, congratulations. You're about to learn more about corporate advertising than anyone's ever collected in one place before. Not just how to do it, although there's plenty of that in here. Not just why to do it, although you'll certainly learn that, too.

The real lesson of this book is how to *think* about corporate advertising.

You'll see examples of 30 of the most successful corporate campaigns ever run; but more important, you'll hear the *thinking* behind the campaigns. From visionary CEOs, like Peter Grace. From legendary creative craftsmen, like David Ogilvy. From the best client ad managers in the business, like Xerox's Michael Kirby.

You'll learn the stories *behind* campaigns you've admired — often surprising stories. You'll learn that what appeared to be soft image advertising often had hard business objectives behind it. You'll hear steely managers dispute the myth that corporate advertising can't be measured, and read the numbers that prove their point. You'll see the real dimensions of corporate advertising, some of which were "integrated marketing communications" programs before there was a word for it.

Everything I thought I knew about corporate advertising would have fit in one chapter of this book (and did!) — but there are nine chapters, which is one measure of how much I learned by reading it.

If you're not an expert on the subject of corporate advertising, after reading this book you will be. If you're already an expert, you'll find as many challenges to your assumptions as you will find evidence supporting your opinions.

Corporate advertising needed this book. I needed this book, twenty years ago; but it hadn't (and couldn't have been) written. *You* need this book, if you have now or ever will have anything to do with corporate advertising.

> Robert F. Lauterborn
> James L. Knight Professor of Advertising
> University of North Carolina at Chapel Hill

Introduction

■ This is a book that I've been wanting to write for some time. Its subject, the use of image advertising to solve certain corporate problems, is one of rapidly growing interest for many marketers. Having developed corporate image campaigns for such diverse clients as banks, industrials, and consumer products companies, I have been deeply aware of and fascinated by this trend.

Image advertising has been with us for a long time, but only began coming into its own in the 1970s and 1980s. The 1990s should by all projections be the "image" decade.

Reasons for this interest are many. A proliferation of mergers, acquisitions, and takeovers . . . deregulation in the financial industry . . . the extraordinary expansion of such new industries as computers and space technology . . . the numbers of overseas companies now seeing the United States as a prime market. All these and more.

One especially valid reason, though not always acknowledged, is that more and more advertisers are beginning to suspect that well-executed corporate image advertising can really help sales and improve a company's bottom line. One of the aims of this book is to substantiate that belief.

Over the past two years, I have surveyed and interviewed many corporate CEOs, marketing and communications directors, agency executives, and business editors. I have had the benefit of their various experiences and insights, and they have made available to me a wealth of case study material on a broad spectrum of landmark image campaigns.

Some of this data was confidential, for my background only. And, obviously, some of the information I have used will lose its immediacy with time. Campaigns that were new when I began this project may no longer be current, while there are many excellent campaigns now running that I have not been able to include for one reason or another.

The book does not attempt to present and critique only what's current in image advertising, however, but rather to explore key aspects of classic image campaigns, both present and past. In this way, we hope to make a real contribution both to the practitioner's and the student's understanding of the subject.

Although my advertising agency, Gregory & Clyburne, has had extensive experience with clients in the image area, I have purposely refrained from including much of this background. I wanted to present as impartial a point of view as possible, and give full credit to the advertising agencies who have created and prepared these campaigns.

The resulting volume proves, I trust, a useful hands-on guide for interested CEOs, COOs, CFOs, marketing and sales executives, advertising and public relations directors, agency executives, and others interested in the development and execution of corporate advertising as the leading edge of tomorrow's marketing.

We will see that no matter what size the corporation, or what its particular image problems, the perceptions held by customers, employees, shareholders, and other audiences play an increasingly important role in its long-term success. They bear a great deal, in fact, on a company's very ability to survive in today's competitive and complex marketplace.

James R. Gregory
Stamford, CT

Acknowledgments

■ The author deeply appreciates all the guidance and support given this project by Casimir Psujek and Anne Knudsen at NTC Publishing Group. I am also grateful to the many advertisers and their agencies who have shared so much of their time and provided so much valuable information for this book, as well as to our many co-workers and friends who have so patiently given advice and encouragement.

I am especially indebted to: Robert Allen, Donald C. Ambuhl, Arlene Anns, Roger Baker, William Bates, Jack Bedell, Robin Bergstrom, Robert Berzok, Frederick E. Bona, Philip A. Bossert, Jerry Brown, Paula Brown, John Caspari, Richard Costello, Rance Crain, Guy Durham, Mary Ann Eger, Tom Failla, Edward A. Faruolo, John Fisher, James Foster, Max J. Friedman, James Garrity, Ronald Geiser, Richard Gelb, Neil D. Gluckin, Kate Gomez, Mary Graham, Robert W. Gunderson, Thomas Haas, Thomas A. Herrmann,

Joseph L. Hickey, Stanley Hironaka, Tamara Homer, Thomas Hoppin, Martha C. Johnson, Arthur C. Kammerman, Maryanne Keller, David N. Kernis, Michael Kirby, John Kriak, J. Dan Lacy, Robert F. Lauterborn, Miranda Lee, Tara Lemmey, Jim Linderman, Douglas Longmire, L. James Lovejoy, Robert M. Lukovics, Leonard Matthews, Thomas D. McCann, John McDonald, David H. Means, Mark J. Minkin, Thomas A. Moore, Edward G. Morrett, Jack Morris, Mary Muenkel, Antonio Navarro, William L. Newkirk, Jaye S. Niefeld, Harry Paster, John Perduyn, William M. Piet, Robert Purcell, Harwood H. Ritter, Dennis A. Ritzel, Bruce Roberts, Ted Rosinski, Stan Rubenstein, Olga Salazar, Michael W. Salius, Charles G. Salmans, Linda M. Scenna, Herb Schmertz, Eugene P. Schonfeld, Sanford C. Schulert, Hank Seiden, Dennis Signorovitch, Rupert Smith, David R. Stivers, Harlan Stone, Mary Ann Sullivan, Robert Swadosh, Lee Tashjian, James Tewksbury, Susan Thomases, Greg Toller, Richard B. White, Richard J. Wiechmann, and Harold Wolfson.

I would be remiss if I did not also include in my thanks the American Association of Advertising Agencies (AAAA), the Association of National Advertisers (ANA), the National Advertising Agency Network (NAAN), and the BBDO Library. All helped greatly in the gathering of necessary facts and data.

Special recognition and appreciation must be given to the Gregory & Clyburne clients who not only helped to make this book possible but provided the principles and inspiration to start it. Among this revered group are: John Adinolfi, Gloria Burke, Nancy Chaikin, Ed Curry, John DiCenzo, Bonnie Elmore, Jack Forde, Barbara Gomard, David Gordon, George V. Grune, Carole M. Howard, Harriett Hull, Frank Jones, Alan Kessman, Craig Lowder, Neil Lyon, Walter Lorenz, Mike Madden, David Maimin, Ted Meredith, Walter Munsen, Hortense Penate, Jim Perakis, Phil Pierucci, Lynn Rutledge, Ed Shufro, Joan Skimmons, Brenda Snyder, Andy Stockton, Mike Teague, Greg Toller, Bruce Trachtenberg, Stanley Walker, Arol Wolford, and Robert Yowell.

A special thank you belongs to the Gregory & Clyburne staff who contributed their time and attention to this long project. Most notable are Jack G. Wiechmann who put the words and concepts to paper, Agnes Conover who transcribed more tapes than she would have preferred, Michael DeBrito for photo research and approvals, Cecile Locurto for compiling the results of our national surveys, Meg Pitts who read the book and filled the holes, and the rest of the staff, C. J. Carpenter, Linda Clasen, Lisa Elliott, Susan Foltin, Ann Gantz, Viki Glover, Evelyn Gregory, Mary Jane Guffey, Cathryn Oulighan, Sharon Scharkss, Lee Ann Schlatter, Santo Spadaro, and Tom Zara.

■ CHAPTER ONE ■

Image:
The Leading Edge of Corporate Strategy

■ Ask a dozen CEOs or marketing executives what corporate image advertising is all about and you get easily a dozen different answers. Or more. That's because image advertising has so many possible missions to so many possible target audiences, and is viewed from so many perspectives.

If you are a CEO you will look at corporate image advertising primarily as a "long haul" tool. If you are the Director of Corporate Communications you may be more interested in its immediate successes.

Whatever the perspective, image advertising, when properly executed, can help dramatically to move the corporation toward meeting corporate goals. It is, in fact, the very leading edge of corporate strategy, essential in positioning a company for maximum growth.

1

In terms of customer relations, image advertising deals mostly with perceptions. We have all heard the saying, "the customer is always right." But with corporate image, it isn't strictly whether the customer is right or wrong that matters. It's what he or she *thinks* about you that counts. Thus every company, even the smallest, has an image, whether planned or not.

Perception Is Reality

Corporate image begins with the public's *perception* of a company—the preconceived ideas and prejudices that have formed in the minds of customers. This perception may not always reflect accurately a corporation's true profile, but to the public it is *reality*. It is up to the CEO especially to be sure those initial impressions are molded into a positive force that will enhance business prospects for the corporation. Or that they are sufficiently changed to match the actuality of the situation.

For example, from its inception Ford was known as a manufacturer of basic, inexpensive transportation for the public. In the late 1970s, negative stories began to circulate about Ford regarding product quality and the company's *perceived* uncaring attitude toward the public.

Ford management decided upon a long-term goal of refurbishing corporate image by establishing product quality as the number one priority for the company. "Quality is Job 1" became the first phase of Ford's new corporate image program.

In-plant quality awareness programs were launched at the same time as a major advertising program. The result was a tremendous surge in the quality of the products manufactured as well as in consumer awareness of Ford as a quality manufacturer. Improved sales followed, and today Ford is sales leader in the U.S. automotive world. Respecting the value of consistency and continuity in successful advertising, Ford still promotes the image of "Quality is Job 1."

Image Advertising as the Least Understood Marketing Tool

The use of corporate image advertising is not a new strategy. It began almost a century ago, with the first real image ads concentrating on the great changes then taking place in the American lifestyle. New inventions such as the automobile, telephone, airplane, and radio were evolving into major industries, and the public needed to be educated as to the reliability and practicality of the new products and the corporations which offered them.

Despite its long history and many documented successes, corporate image advertising remains the least understood tool in the marketing kit today. Different people approach it in different ways, for different reasons, expecting different kinds of results.

How to best utilize image advertising is the subject of this book. The following chapters cover its basic missions, examine pertinent case history material, and suggest ways you can utilize image advertising to strengthen your company. The case studies are of mostly large corporations and banks, but the lessons to be learned are just as valuable for the small company as for a member of the Fortune 500.

Over the years the author has witnessed the positive effects well-conceived image campaigns can have on businesses. We have also noted the many mistaken ideas some executives have regarding the whole subject of image. For example, there is a common belief that dollars used to enhance corporate image will ultimately be taken from product advertising, to the detriment of sales. This all-too-frequent point of view is evidenced clearly by a recent survey, made specifically for this book, of members of the National Advertising Agency Network (NAAN). When asked about client attitudes toward corporate image advertising, a significant number of responding agencies claimed the words ''image advertising'' are a red flag to salespeople, a definite pitfall to be avoided. One agency wrote: ''Such phrasing means 'no sale' to the sales people . . . fluffy stuff, no real teeth. We avoid the use of that term as if it were the plague.''

When this attitude permeates a corporation, it is difficult to promote image programs. Fortunately, more and more experienced marketers now recognize the advantages of strong, timely corporate advertising. They understand that in the long term, properly spent, those corporate image dollars can indeed help *increase brand sales* as well as accomplish other important tasks.

A Burgeoning Business

Although the major portion of ad budget dollars still goes into brand or product promotion, corporate image advertising expenditures are growing by leaps and bounds. According to the Association of National Advertisers (ANA), image advertising is a burgeoning business, with more than half of the larger U.S. companies using advertising to promote ideas as well as products.

As recently as 25 years ago it would have seemed impossible for U.S. corporations *in total* to ever spend as much as $50 million a year on image advertising. In 1989 the figure was well over 600 million, and it keeps growing. On an individual company basis, the latest ANA Corporate Advertising Practices study shows the average annual corporate advertising budget in 1990 to have risen to $7.9 million, up two percent from 1989.

Why this tremendous and rapid growth? One reason is the soaring number of mergers, acquisitions, divestitures, and takeovers which continue to change the corporate scene drastically. They alter both the *realities* of the companies involved and the *perceptions* of those companies held by their various publics. Added to this confusion on the corporate scene are the recent deregulation of banks and other financial institutions and the invasion of European and Asian advertisers into the U.S. media.

When current images are made obsolete, customers, shareholders, employees, and others begin to wonder about a company's products, its profits, its direction, and its future. Clearly they need to be told what has happened, what is happening, and what is going to happen. A corporation undergoing important changes needs to present its new reality to its public and needs to create a new environment for up-to-date perceptions.

The Mission of Image Advertising

Although experts may disagree as to the exact number, there are at least seven basic missions for image advertising. Properly conceived and implemented, image advertising can be the leading edge of corporate strategy for your company, helping to:

1. Build public awareness and acceptance and establish a more favorable market position.

2. Redefine your corporation after a merger, takeover, acquisition, or name change.

3. Pre-sell target markets to support product marketing.

4. Influence shareholders and the financial community.

5. Establish your company's position on timely issues.

6. Assist in the management of a crisis situation.

7. Attract and hold quality employees, while creating a cooperative environment in their communities.

Whatever the mission, an image campaign should be market-driven and should have specific objectives. Those objectives may often apply to more than one mission. In other words, a campaign to announce a name change can do much more than merely make an announcement. It can also make the general public more aware of the corporation and its strengths, generate interest in company brands, pass along important information to the financial community, and influence potential employees.

Three Basic Ingredients for Success

What makes for successful image advertising? Whatever the mission, three factors are almost always involved:

1. *Direction or focus.* Have you done the necessary research to articulate your corporate mission . . . to set the right goals . . . to know the audience(s) you must influence . . . to select the media to best reach your target publics?

2. *Creativity.* Will your advertising really ''cut through the clutter'' . . . be noticed . . . be remembered . . . be acted upon?

3. *Consistency.* Will your campaign run long enough to have real value . . . will all of your advertising carry the same theme, support the same message, even abroad?

Other factors, of course, may seem equally important in given situations. Even so, these three basic ingredients, properly implemented, are a sure recipe for a workable image campaign that gets results. In the remainder of this chapter we will examine them each in turn.

Establish Your Direction or Focus

President Harry Truman used to keep a plaque on his desk which read: The Buck Stops Here. He understood that there was really only one person responsible for leading the nation, and he was it.

In image advertising it's the responsibility of the CEO to determine the campaign's mission, or missions, what new image is required, and later judge whether set goals are being met.

David Ogilvy, who has been responsible for more successful corporate campaigns than anyone can probably remember, said in reference to a campaign created by his agency for IBM:

Every commercial and every advertisement we did had to be submitted to Tom Watson and his brother, Dick, at the top. It was all done at the top level. I think that's just as it should be.

It's a waste of money for any corporation to do corporate advertising unless they define the purpose of that advertising. In my judgment . . . it should be defined by the head of your corporation—for three reasons:

If you get the top man to define the purpose, he's more likely to keep the campaign going. Corporate campaigns which don't have the personal involvement of the chief executive don't last long . . .

"The top man in your company is the only person who is in a position to reconcile the conflicting purposes of the different departments in the company . . .

"Only the top man in a company can find enough money to do the job . . ."[1]

Part of the job description of the top man in any corporation should be to define the corporation's purpose, and to define it in such a way that will be relevant far into the future. In this manner, corporate advertising—unlike brand advertising—becomes the voice of the chief executive and his or her board of directors.

Whether or not the CEO actually initiates the corporate campaign, it is the CEO who is held responsible by the board and shareholders for its ultimate success or failure. Thus an involved CEO will give the program active guidance and a strong sense of direction. The CEO must know and define, at least in some general sense, what specific problem needs to be solved, and how the solution is to be developed.

Focus is crucial because an image campaign can have significant impact on more than one area of the company. The primary objective should be an extension of long-term corporate strategy, directed at those aspects of the business that hinder the company from fully achieving corporate goals.

If, for example, the problem is one of stock undervaluation, the CEO needs to decide whose opinion he or she wants to influence, how to influence that opinion, how much the company should spend to reach the goal, and to what extent he or she wants to be involved personally in the program's implementation.

Or perhaps the company has just gone through an acquisition or merger, calling for a new name and logo. The CEO may choose to spearhead the development of an appropriate new identity and announce the change in person to the corporation's target markets.

---

[1] From a speech given to *Fortune* Corporate Communications Seminar, Saint-Paul-de-Vence, France; June 7–10, 1978.

Choose Your Target Carefully

The target market for image advertising is known as the "corporate audience." It consists of "those people who are capable of assimilating a corporate message and who are willing to consider more than one position before making up their minds on an issue or problem. [They] generally fall into four groups. Business leaders. Activists. The financial community. Government leaders."[2]

Customers and prospects, employees and potential employees, investors, and the trade are also prime targets for many advertisers. Don't overlook the media itself. It's important that their perceptions of your company correspond with the corporate image you wish to promote. This is doubly true if you are involved with the management of some crisis situation.

The selection of just the right audience—or combination of audiences—depends upon strategy and mission. Whatever your goal, image advertising gives your company an unmatched opportunity to present a particular point of view, exactly as you wish to communicate it, to precisely the right people.

Listen to what *Grey Matter* says:

"The gravity of decisions now being made in board rooms across the U.S. makes it imperative that the lines of communication between corporations and their various publics be kept open . . . Through corporate campaigns companies disseminate information, generate support, increase awareness, correct misconceptions, and create goodwill. Moreover, only through corporate advertising can companies publicly express their uncensored, unedited views about the society in which they operate and the events that affect their prosperity."[3]

Chrysler—Landmark Image Program

These "uncensored, unedited views" usually originate in the CEO's office, but at the least they should have his or her complete approval and backing.

Certainly one of the more memorable of such corporate campaigns was the program the floundering Chrysler Corporation mounted in the early 1980s in its life-and-death struggle to turn itself around from the brink of bankruptcy. Here was a case of the CEO, Lee Iaccoca, not only determining the mission of his corporate advertising, but also being deeply and personally involved in its creation and execution.

Iaccoca did not work in a vacuum. He utilized the advertising expertise of his

---

[2]From "Why Corporate Advertising," a marketing report by *Time*, 1983.
[3]*Grey Matter,* Vol. 54, No. 2, 1983. Courtesy of Grey Advertising.

people, and also invited his newly appointed advertising agency, Kenyon & Eckhardt, to become a full marketing partner of Chrysler. In effect, the agency was to serve as the company's marketing department during this difficult time of corporate rebirth. K&E was given permanent representation on two important corporate committees: Marketing and Product Planning, as well as serving temporarily on several others—an opportunity seldom offered to an agency!

The result of this unique partnership was a corporate program that was, to a large degree, responsible for what *Time* magazine called a "modern management miracle."

Chrysler had lost a whopping $3.5 billion during the period from 1978–81. This record-breaking loss was due in large part to soaring gasoline prices, coupled with the so-called "small car revolution" in the nation's car-buying habits. Chrysler was left with 200,000 full-size cars in inventory.

Cash—or the lack of it—was Chrysler's single biggest problem. The company looked to Congress for a $1 billion loan guarantee to supply the cash it needed. The general public, along with many members of Congress, believed that Chrysler was looking for a handout, when actually all the company asked for was a credit rating of the same sort routinely granted to many others.

The media didn't help. The press gave the impression that taxpayers' dollars would be used to bail out Chrysler. They insisted on calling the loan a subsidy and claimed that it went against the system of free enterprise. They even implied that it was only right, under the circumstances, for Chrysler to go down the drain.

Chrysler needed an effective, reliable method of projecting to its various publics uncensored viewpoints regarding the difficult situation in which it found itself. The answer lay in image advertising, with a major campaign which was, in effect, "paid-for PR." They used the media to tell the corporation's side of the story with a message that was free of any editorial change, comment, or interpretation.

At that time, Iaccoca was acting as the leading spokesman for his company before Congressional and Senate hearings in Washington. Resulting publicity was valuable, but by itself could not maintain the confidence of the automobile buyer. Sales were dropping drastically because consumers didn't dare buy cars from a company that might not be around to service them. In fact, the percentage of potential customers who were willing even to consider buying a Chrysler-made automobile dropped to only 13 percent from a previous 30 percent.

Chrysler Goes to the People

K&E strongly recommended going to the people with the real facts of the case. Iaccoca agreed and worked with the agency to produce a series of ads that would reassure the public about Chrysler's future.

Quoting Iaccoca in his best-selling autobiography, "We had to let people know two things—first, that we had absolutely no intention of going out of business, and second, that we were making the kind of cars America really needed.''[4]

Instead of their usual product advertising, Chrysler ran editorial-style ads outlining the company's long-range plans and expressing the company's point of view about the loan guarantees. These ads exposed some of the more prevalent myths about Chrysler, pointing out that: they were *not* building gas-guzzlers, they were *not* asking Washington for a handout, and that loan guarantees for Chrysler did *not* set a dangerous precedent.

The ads that Chrysler ran were unusual in their frankness. Instead of ignoring the bad press it was receiving, the company met it head-on and countered the negative stories with facts. For example, one ad carried the heading: ''Would America be better off without Chrysler?'', articulating what many people were beginning to wonder. The ad answered the question with truthful information that had not been readily available to the general public.

Other ads in the series were headlined:

- Doesn't everyone know that Chrysler cars get lousy gas mileage?

- Aren't Chrysler's big cars too big?

- Isn't Chrysler building the wrong kind of cars?

- Is Chrysler management strong enough to turn the company around?

- Has Chrysler done everything it can to help itself?

- Does Chrysler have a future?

Common to all of the ads is the editorial style and the unusually long copy. Chrysler had a story to tell and felt sure the American people would read it. Large numbers of them did.

According to Iaccoca, ''These ads were unusual in another way, too. We decided they should all carry my signature . . . after all, a chief executive of a company that's going broke has to reassure people. He's got to say: 'I'm here, I'm real, and I'm responsible for this company'.''

That the advertising campaign was a resounding success is history. It had real impact on the general public, who could now read Chrysler's side of the story in the same newspapers whose headlines proclaimed doom and gloom about the corporation. Perhaps even more important, Iaccoca believes that the ads played a substantial role in convincing Congress to finally approve the all-important loan guarantees.

---

[4]*Iaccoca*, Lee Iaccoca, Bantam Books, New York, 1984.

Television Aids Credibility

During the hearings Iaccoca had become a well-known figure, and Chrysler was constantly in the news. To capitalize still further on this national exposure, Kenyon & Eckhardt recommended that he appear in a series of TV commercials. There were many still who believed the company was going bankrupt, and only Iaccoca himself could set them straight.

At first Iaccoca delivered only tag lines at the ends of the commercials, such as: "I'm not asking you to buy one of our cars on faith. I'm asking you to compare." As the campaign evolved, the approach grew more aggressive. A perfect example of this new boldness was the now famous line: "If you can find a better car—buy it," with Iaccoca pointing his finger at the camera.

The company was already perceived by the public as being very different from the rest of the American auto industry. Chrysler could try to join the crowd or it could accept a separate identity and make it work to its advantage. By featuring the CEO actively in commercials, Chrysler chose the latter course.

Up to that time the general feeling by the public had been that German and Japanese cars were basically better than anything coming out of Detroit. The television commercials, as the Iaccoca-signed print ads that preceded them, dealt directly with consumers' many doubts and reservations, not only regarding Chrysler but about all American-made automobiles.

Iaccoca projected a spirit of confidence in Chrysler, and planted the thought in the customer's mind that he or she should at least consider a Chrysler. Iaccoca believed that the quality of Chrysler cars would be evident to anyone who checked. Sales were bound to increase if they could only get the customers into the showrooms. That, of course, is exactly what happened.

However, time has passed since that dramatic turnaround, and Chrysler once again has fallen on hard times. Although Iaccoca has appeared sporadically in recent television commercials, the question remains: Would Chrysler have done better to have kept the original Iaccoca campaign going?

Antonio Navarro tells of another strong corporate leader, J. Peter Grace, Chairman of the W.R. Grace Company. The mission of his corporate program was to influence legislation on capital gains. How the campaign helped reduce taxation on capital gains from 49 percent to 28 percent will be detailed in Chapter 6, but consider Navarro's comments on the role of a strong CEO. "It's obvious that such advertising must have the endorsement of the company's chief executive. In fact, it must have more than his endorsement. It must originate with the sincere concern of the top executive or it simply won't work."[5]

---

[5]From "Industry Feature/Corporate Advertising: W. R. Grace & Co.," an interview with Antonio Navarro, Madison Avenue, February 1979.

SUPPOSE THE CEO ISN'T PERSONALLY INVOLVED

What if the CEO doesn't provide any special sense of mission, and cannot clearly define corporate purpose or goals? Can a corporate campaign succeed under these conditions?

It's possible, of course, but chances are the task at hand will be that much harder. Consider the case of one large industrial company that did mount a successful and rather complex corporate program despite a lack of leadership from the top.

Formerly a part of a well-known conglomerate, the company had been purchased by a lesser-known corporation, resulting in a major identity crisis with customers and prospects as well as with employees. The latter, upset by the changes, were beginning to leave the company in sizable numbers.

The new CEO agreed that it was a good time to launch a corporate campaign, but could offer no specific rationale or direction. Instead he turned the problem over to his marketing director, who, happily, was both experienced and innovative.

With the CEO's approval, the marketing director asked our advertising agency to help establish appropriate objectives for the campaign. After researching target publics and employees, we decided upon the following:

1. To announce to all targets the new corporate name and logo;

2. To present to customers, prospects, and the financial community the company's breadth of capability and potential for success; and

3. To counteract any misgivings employees might have regarding the sale of the company and the resultant management changes.

We began with a corporate identity program that featured the consolidation of several divisional logos—each with its own history and design peculiarities—into one new corporate logo that could be accepted by all divisions.

The next step was the development of an image campaign highlighting the company's many special capabilities in a number of totally unrelated markets. Covering a wide diversity of product applications, we prepared a full-color campaign. Each ad represented a division, but tied these separate operations into a single corporation with visual consistency from ad to ad.

Follow-through materials included new packaging, a corporate capabilities brochure, and a special brochure announcing the new logo and showing the new image ads and their media schedule.

Presented with the proposed plan, the CEO committed himself to it fully. As the program rolled out, it became obvious that we had a winner in all respects. Even employees reacted positively, and defections slowed, then stopped. The

CEO had not supplied the usual guidance but does deserve credit for allowing his corporate communications team to move ahead freely.

When direction is clearly understood and defined by the CEO in the first place and an experienced team is given the latitude to work intelligently and with imagination, even the most difficult challenge is made a lot easier.

Creativity and Consistency

IF YOUR ADS AREN'T GOOD, NOTHING MAY HAPPEN

The great problem with corporate advertising—as with product advertising—is that so much of it is done so badly. And if the ads aren't any good, nothing much may happen.

Most people, even many in the advertising business, don't really know the difference between good advertising and bad. They don't understand why one ad might sell ten or fifteen times as much as another for the same product. That's a very real difference.

There are those advertisers that fail to define the purpose of their corporate advertising, or they may assign too many purposes to it. Or they may not identify their target audience accurately or completely. Very often, too, they make the mistake of not measuring results. They fly blind. How then can they possibly know for sure how effective their corporate advertising is?

DAVID OGILVY'S FOUR CAVEATS FOR CREATIVE EXCELLENCE

There is, of course, no formula for creative excellence. But there are certain guidelines to follow, certain pitfalls to beware of. David Ogilvy puts it this way:

> Corporation advertising should not insult the intelligence of the public. It should be plainspoken, candid, adult, honest, intelligent, and specific. It should avoid preachment or self-congratulation. It should be rooted in products or capabilities or service or policies. It should be interesting . . . you cannot bore people into admiring your company.
>
> Corporate advertising requires creative genius to penetrate the indifference with which people regard most corporations. If nobody reads the

message . . . except you, nothing is going to happen. You can't save souls in an empty church.[6]

How W.R. Grace Got Extra Mileage

Corporate advertising often focuses on a product or service in some positive manner. Ads even tend to be boastful, which is perfectly all right in that context, the only problem being that just about everybody else is doing it. Advertisers often seem to forget they are competing with many peer corporations, primarily in magazines where it's just one image ad after another.

Antonio Navarro, Senior Vice President of W.R. Grace, puts it this way:

> "An excellent way to stand out is to have exceptionally good advertising. We discovered that if we spent the *same* money, but tackled a national issue in which we could be perceived as having an enlightened self-interest as well as concern for the community and nation, we would get more mileage for our advertising dollar. Witness the 'baby' ad."

Shown on the following page in print form, this strong message on the nation's deficit features a baby starting life saddled with a $50,000 share of the national debt. The print version offers the headline: She's got her mother's eyes, her father's nose and her uncle's deficit. The striking color photograph shows "Uncle Sam" holding a small baby. Copy is crisp and informative.

The ad made it unsolicited into the news pages of the *New York Times* and was covered as a news event by other major newspapers and leading magazines. Navarro estimates that the ad received well over $1 million worth of free publicity by being discussed on TV alone. And in a single month, 62,000 people responded to the telephone number mentioned in the commercial (1–800–USA––DEBT), requesting a copy of an informative brochure.

Nor was this ad a one-shot wonder, but part of a total effort that was highly successful in bringing the name of W.R. Grace to the attention of the American people. We'll cover this unique advertising program, and its predecessor, in a later chapter. Obviously W.R. Grace's approach to image advertising isn't the

---

[6]From a speech given to *Fortune* Corporate Communications Seminar, Saint-Paul-de-Vence, France, June 7–10, 1978.

SHE'S GOT HER MOTHER'S EYES, HER FATHER'S NOSE AND HER UNCLE'S DEFICIT.

It's quite a legacy her uncle has handed her. (Her favorite uncle, at that.) Annual federal deficits approaching $200 billion. A current national debt of $1.6 trillion. Potentially, $13 trillion by the year 2000.

When the numbers get this big, they tend to get meaningless. Until you look at it this way. If federal deficits continue at their current rate, it's as if every baby born in 1985 will have a $50,000 debt strapped to its back.

The great debate over deficits, of course, no longer centers on whether or not they should be reduced, but how.

One side favors raising taxes. But whose? 90% of all personal taxable income already comes from tax brackets of $35,000 and below. Does anyone seriously suggest increasing the tax burden of lower and middle income families?

Well then, the argument follows, tax the rich. But, if the federal government took every penny of every dollar over the $75,000 tax bracket that isn't already taxed—not

a surcharge, mind you, but took it all—it would only collect enough to run the country for a week. Besides, there's no guarantee that Congress would spend less money if we all gave them more.

The alternative seems clear. Cut spending. But, again, the question is how.

We're W.R. Grace & Co. While our business interests in chemicals, natural resources and consumer

services are worldwide, our primary interest is in the future of America's economy. That's where any corporation's best interest lies.

To that end, our chairman headed a presidential commission that identified ways to end abuses in federal spending. It found 2,478 ways. Specific ways.

The President has seen the report. So has Congress. We think you should know what they

know. There's a booklet that summarizes it all. For your free copy, write to this address: USA DEBT, Dept. U, P.O. Box 3190, Ogden, Utah 84409.

Unfortunately, almost 75% of the commission's recommendations won't be implemented unless Congress acts on them. And, sometimes, the words "Congressional action" are mutually exclusive. That's why we all have to take action first.

Read the booklet. If it gets you angry, it's up to you to get things changed. Write to Congress. If you don't think that'll do it, run for Congress.

Our children and grandchildren don't deserve to pay for our mistakes. We should be passing on to them a healthy economy and a high standard of living. That should be their inheritance. That should be their birthright.

GRACE
One step ahead
of a changing world.

W.R. Grace & Co., 1114 Avenue of the Americas, New York, NY 10036.

Courtesy of W. R. Grace & Co.

only one. The point is that thoughtful, creative advertising can cut through clutter, touch a nerve, and make things happen.

Many Forms, Many Themes, Many Media

Successful image advertising comes in many styles and shapes. Long, editorial copy or short, selling copy. Photography, illustration, or all-type. Inserts, spreads, single pages, and even fractional units. Color or black-and-white. In just about every combination possible, and in a bewildering assortment of business, trade, and consumer magazines and newspapers. And don't forget the electronic media.

Some campaigns feature products or services; some talk about capabilities or markets served; still others establish corporate philosophy. Whatever the format, whatever the theme, whatever the media, each image campaign featured in this book was carefully, even lovingly, conceived and executed. All have been successful in their own way; and while some may seem more "creative" than others—beauty is in the eye of the beholder—all worked, and there's a lesson to be learned from each.

Although there's no formula that guarantees great ads, there are three questions, the answers to which can lead to good corporate as well as good product advertising. Hank Seiden, chairman of Ketchum Advertising and a top creative man in his own right, has this to say in *Advertising Age:*

> Whenever I see lousy advertising, I try to analyze why I think it's lousy. This . . . has not only helped me understand what makes advertising bad but, more importantly, how to make it good. It all comes down to three questions. While answering all three . . . doesn't guarantee great advertising, it at least assures reasonably good advertising.
>
> The first question is *Who?*—Who are you talking to? . . . Demand a detailed description of the target audience. The better you know your customers, the better you can sell them.
>
> The second question is *What?*—What do you say to them? You're looking for that one salient appeal . . . Only the *Who?* people know for sure, so ask them. Good research leads to good advertising.
>
> Answering the third question first is the single biggest reason for third-rate advertising. The question is *How?*—How do you say it? Execution makes or breaks advertising. It can break it if you haven't answered the first two questions before [the third].
>
> These three questions should lead to good advertising, which I define as the right execution of the right appeal to the right audience.[7]

---

[7]"The Three Most Important Questions in Advertising," Hank Seiden, *Advertising Age,* May 1, 1989.

Citibank:
Meeting a Changing Market

Just as life a couple of generations ago was a lot simpler than it is today, so too were the marketing challenges faced by First National City Bank far less complex than those now confronting Citicorp.

Consumers today are bombarded with countless advertising messages, many of which don't even attempt to explain the products, services, or companies behind them. The marketplace becomes increasingly complicated and confusing, and the traditionally staid financial services market is no exception.

Little wonder there is a competitive crisis in banking. Little wonder Citicorp saw a need for a national image campaign if it was to succeed in this new, constantly changing financial services environment.

Nor is Citicorp's competition limited to other giant banks. Says Mary Ann Eger, bank vice president, "We are beset on all sides by non-bank competitors. It is a legal and regulatory dilemma, but we see it as far more important for its competitive significance. It's a roll call of companies lining up to get into our business."

Expansion of the Non-Banks

It's easy to understand Citicorp's concern. Both General Motors and Ford actively pursue the retail financing business. They have vast experience with credit, and their databases are filled with credit-worthy prospective customers. Other top national competitors include Amex, Merrill Lynch, Prudential, and Sears Financial Network.

Many of these non-bank competitors have consistently and substantially increased their advertising expenditures. In fact, 80 percent of the advertising dollars spent in the financial services category in 1987 was spent by non-banks. As Ms. Eger says, "A lot of people are interested in getting a piece of our business."

A Major Opportunity

Research, completed before Citicorp launched its image campaign, indicated that many consumers believed Sears was the leading financial services innovator, however, 45 percent of the respondents "didn't really know." Sears was also perceived to be the leader in meeting consumers' financial needs, but, again, many respondents were not sure.

Those "don't knows" and "not sures" presented a major opportunity for Citicorp.

The fact was that few people in the marketplace were aware that Citicorp/Citibank was actually the largest bank in the country as well as the nation's largest financial services company. Nor were they aware that Citicorp is a global company with 90,000 employees, in 2,900 locations, in 42 states and 90 countries, or that Citicorp was already doing business with one in five American families, was the largest marketer of student loans, and the largest servicer of home mortgages.

If Citicorp was going to continue to grow, the company needed to change perceptions. To continue as a marketing leader, the company had to become a leader in communication as well. It was a made-to-order environment for a national image campaign. There was a marked need to build awareness of the Citicorp name, heritage, and commitment to customers, as well as acceptance of its products and services.

THE ESSENTIAL INGREDIENT

Two interrelated goals were agreed upon. First, to establish relationships with consumers nationally, and second, to become their preferred provider of a broad range of financial services.

The essential ingredient in establishing a strong consumer relationship is communications. Advertising leading to overall awareness becomes the very foundation of this relationship-building. It is the first contact with the consumer. Get prospective customers to buy the company, and then they'll buy the product.

DIFFERENTIATE THE BANK

Ms. Eger comments on Citicorp's creative approach to the task: "With our agency, N.W. Ayer, we agreed that the advertising should clearly differentiate the bank from the competition. It should introduce Citicorp and Citibank in a distinctive manner and develop widespread awareness of the company as the nation's number one financial services organization, ready to help consumers achieve a wide range of financial and life goals."

The campaign was built around two main elements: A theme line—"Citicorp. Because Americans want to succeed, not just survive,"—and a graphic—the Citicorp Building.

"We believe," says Eger, "that the theme line captures an essential part of the American spirit. It also reflects an attitude that we share as a company, and that has contributed to our own corporate success. New York's Citi-corp Center Building is a logical extension of our 'success' concept.

"Because of its unique design, it is an appropriate symbol, a powerful representation of Citicorp's size and capability. Both elements do much to help set us apart from the crowd in a cluttered marketplace."

In order to confirm the wisdom of their creative judgment, Citicorp did some research. The company wanted to be sure the concept did not connote a "Big, bad, New York money center bank" image. It was found instead that the con-cept actually supported the strategic thrust of the campaign—it communicated that Citicorp is a large, successful, progressive company.

Citicorp also pretested magazine layouts and TV photomatics. The research confirmed that the theme line reflected how Americans feel about themselves and their heritage. Post-testing showed that the advertising clearly communi-cated the Citicorp message. In other words, key corporate attribute ratings such as "large," "successful," "innovative," "substantial," and "helpful" were significantly increased among those exposed to the advertising.

LET THE EMPLOYEES KNOW

In September, 1987, the bank introduced the new advertising to a gathering of Citicorp Senior Management from around the world. Simultaneously, the bank distributed 20,000 communications kits to Citicorp and Citibank man-agers throughout the country in order for the whole company to understand the program and feel part of the effort. For maximum impact, the campaign was launched on September 14th, during the ABC telecast of the New York Giants–Chicago Bears football game. The company continued building momentum by dropping spots into the World Series telecasts.

RETAIL STRATEGY

In New York, Citibank has translated its corporate image idea into retail strat-egy. The promise becomes: "Citibank—When, Where and How to Succeed." The award-winning advertising emphasizes the theme of access to the bank's products, services, energy, ideas, and people.

The success theme has also been used by various Citicorp businesses around the country, and has been adapted for the annual and quarterly reports as well as for a college recruitment effort.

Ms. Eger concludes:

"The battle for share of mind among consumers and businesses is intense. Our campaign didn't happen in 60 or 90 days or even in 12–18 months for that matter. It was a long and at times arduous process.

"But the end result was a national image campaign that positions Citicorp as a leading financial services company. The advertising supports our lines of business; it links both Citicorp and Citibank. The concept and theme position Citicorp with what Americans believe about themselves. They also begin the process of positioning Citicorp/Citibank as a communications leader."

A final note: Recent turmoil in the banking industry has persuaded Citicorp/Citibank to cut back on jobs and staff. It will be interesting to see what part image advertising will play for them in the current banking crisis.

DU PONT—OLDEST LIVING CORPORATE CAMPAIGN?

To be honest, I don't know which the oldest example of a corporate campaign, still in service, might be. But Du Pont's is certainly right up there—a perfect example of not trying to fix what isn't broken!

Du Pont's advertising strategy was born in 1935 and still survives today. Originally designed for radio, Du Pont's corporate image program has appeared on television for the past 35 years, and recently has also utilized print. All this time Du Pont has used corporate communications to achieve one objective: to teach the American public the real nature of its business, creating a favorable image for a long line of products with very limited public visibility.

This corporate program got its start under the stimulus of rather severe negative publicity that surrounded a U.S. Senate investigation of alleged World War I profiteers. This was the so-called "merchants of death" investigation conducted by the Nye Committee in 1935.

Now, Du Pont in truth had been a major supplier of military explosives to the British and French governments during World War I, making some very large profits as a result. But following the war this business had shrunk substantially, with military explosives accounting for less than one percent of Du Pont's sales.

The company, in 1935, was a giant without any visible identity except for the public's memories of them as "merchants of death." Roy Durstine, then creative director at Batten, Barton, Durstine & Osborn, took note of this and made the company a twofold proposal. First he suggested the creation and sponsorship of a weekly radio show, dramatizing incidents in U.S. history, to be called "Cavalcade of America."

Then he proposed the slogan: Better Things for Better Living. Du Pont, adding the words "Through Chemistry" to the slogan, liked the concept and bought the package. "Cavalcade of America" became a weekly prime-time network radio show and Du Pont's face to the world, and remained so until 1953 when Du Pont left radio for television.

For 18 years Du Pont had advertised low-visibility, unfamiliar products on prime-time network radio, not to sell the products but simply to explain what Du Pont did for a living. The program demonstrated that the reach and frequency of network radio in those days could promote unglamorous products successfully and build public favorability.

In 1937 only 47 percent of the adult American public had a favorable impression of Du Pont. Twenty years later the figure was 79 percent and continues at that kind of level today. The numbers are credible because Du Pont researched the reputational impact of "Cavalcade" year after year using a very large national sample. Careful research has always been a hallmark of Du Pont's corporate advertising, and to this day they spend liberally in this area.

"Cavalcade of America" left radio in the spring of 1953 and became a television program. The medium changed, but the advertising strategy did not. Interesting product information, using a problem/solution/result format, was the backbone of Du Pont's corporate strategy in the 1930s and continues to be more than half a century later.

Du Pont Combines Focus, Product, and Emotion

That strategy today is made up of three elements. First, Du Pont wants to focus on significant public issues. The company works hard to identify the things that people really care about, the problems that concern society most. Topics such as disability awareness, breast cancer, AIDS, automotive safety. The people at Du Pont believe that when members of the public watch one of the company's television commercials or read a magazine ad, they will relate quickly and directly to the subject matter if it involves a public concern.

Next, Du Pont selects products to feature that connect in a constructive, positive way with one of these major public issues. With more than 1,800 products, Du Pont has a lot of choices.

Finally, they build emotion into their advertising. Many advertisers want only to communicate large volumes of information. Du Pont wants you to *feel* something. In perhaps their most recognized commercial, Du Pont wants you to see and be touched by a disabled veteran, Bill Denby, playing basketball. And millions of Americans have responded.

Perhaps this particular commercial needs special attention. Bill Denby lost both legs to a land mine in Vietnam. He is a real person who had real dreams of playing pro basketball. Bill's own courage and determination, supported by prosthetic legs made from Du Pont products, have created the miracle you see on the screen—Bill Denby playing basketball, hard and well.

Talk about impact! Bill has been on almost every major radio and television news program you can think of. He has been featured on CBS Sports, ABC

Sports, and NBC Sports programs, and was named "Sportsman of the Year" by the *Chicago Sun-Times*. The commercial itself won a CLIO in 1988, and is generally considered the best thing that Du Pont has ever done in the way of corporate advertising.

Don't Stop the Steady Flow of Information

Quoting Lee Tashjian, Du Pont's Managing Director of Public Affairs:

> Corporate advertising has been Du Pont's primary vehicle of public visibility. The majority of (our) products enjoy no public visibility whatsoever except through the medium of corporate advertising. Yet these products are essential to the world's living standards. Research has shown that public attitudes toward the company are favorably influenced by a continuing flow of information about the Company and its products.
>
> I must stress the word 'continuing.' Continuity has been essential because image building is a slow and cumulative process. If the process is interrupted the cumulative gains of many years tend to evaporate very, very quickly. I repeat, continuity is absolutely essential in our view to cost efficiency.

Looking back at Du Pont's 50-plus years of corporate advertising, it is striking to note that the more things change the more they are the same. The words may be different, the products featured may be different, but the message is always the same: Du Pont makes the things that make a difference. Better Things for Better Living still—even though corporate growth and diversification have resulted in dropping the phrase "Through Chemistry."

Now that's consistency—both in continuity and in theme!

Familiarity Leads to Favorability—at Home and Abroad

Like many other major U.S. corporations, Du Pont has become a global company in the last 30 years. Although perhaps somewhat slow to employ full-scale corporate advertising outside the U.S., Du Pont is now making significant progress. In Japan, for example, the company has instituted a major corporate print campaign aimed at business executives and professionals. At the campaign's start in 1984, Du Pont's effective awareness was about 21 percent. Today the familiarity level is in the range of 30 percent. And each increase in awareness has been accompanied by a significant increase in favorability.

Encouraged by success in Japan, Du Pont has initiated a major print campaign in Germany and has plans to expand the program into France, Italy, and the United Kingdom, as well as into other Far Eastern nations.

Says Tashjian:

Tens of thousands of customers have come to know Du Pont much better through our corporate advertising. We have always subscribed to the theory that familiarity and favorability are inseparably linked. Our experience seems to validate that theory. There is reason to believe that the [strategy] that has served us so well in the United States will also serve us equally well worldwide.

We'll touch on this again in Chapter 9.

Six Guides to Success

We have seen that all corporate image advertising is not alike. Different companies have different problems, different needs, and perceive the marketplace—and the world—through different eyes.

In the creation and preparation of almost every successful image campaign, however, certain basic guides are generally followed. These are:

1. *Perception* is what counts; it's not necessarily the reality of a situation but what your target audience *believes to be reality* that creates corporate image.

2. *Direction* for an image campaign should be established at the top—usually by the CEO. He or she is the only one who understands the company from all viewpoints, can employ personal involvement toward reconciling conflicts between divisions and departments, can keep the campaign going on track, and can find the necessary budget to get the job done.

3. *Know Thyself.* You've got to know who you are before you can decide where you're going. What is your image? Do you need an image campaign at all? Some companies don't, of course. In other words, employ research: before, during, and after any image program.

4. *Focus.* Do you know *who* you are trying to reach? The better you understand your audience(s), the better you can influence their perceptions of your company.

5. *Creativity. What* will your campaign say to its target publics? What single specific appeal will best "cut through the clutter," be remembered and acted upon? Study your audience; they are the only ones who can provide the answer.

6. *Consistency.* It goes hand in hand with creativity. The execution of your advertising, or the *how* of it, must be dependent upon the answers to *who* and *what.* By nature it must involve not only consistency of theme but also of exposure, or your entire investment may be wasted.

Let's examine how the four corporations featured in this chapter have utilized these guides.

Ford established a *long-term program,* focusing on the *single message of quality.* Negative public *perceptions were changed* to help increase the sale of product and bring the company back to the number one position in its field.

Chrysler, actively *led by its* charismatic *CEO,* took the bull by the horns and focused on its own problems. *Unusually frank ads* and TV commercials featuring CEO Iaccoca appealed to the auto-buying general public and helped the company turn itself around by *changing both consumer and governmental attitudes.* Chrysler received its much-needed financing and began to sell its products again. The happy ending: Chrysler repaid the entire amount, plus interest.

W.R. Grace, *directed by its own* dynamic *CEO,* got more mileage for its corporate image dollars by concentrating on *compelling national issues* such as the national debt. Thoughtful, creative ads cut through clutter, touched nerves, and *made things happen.* Specifically, it brought a whole *new and more complete perception* of W.R. Grace to its customers, shareholders, employees, and to the general public.

Du Pont's *long-running, single focus strategy* has done much to *create a positive perception* for many heretofore "invisible" products by giving them valuable public exposure, using familiarity to create acceptance and favorability and to make sales.

"THE MEDIUM IS THE MESSAGE"[8]

Before going on to talk about some of the specific missions of corporate image advertising, we must point out in advance that a company's image is a composite of *all* of its actions—including communications.

In a recent interview, Harwood Ritter, Manager of Corporate Marketing Communications for Ethyl Corporation, put it this way:

How a company communicates is very much a part of what it does. All internal and external communications produced for a company contribute to its image by both demonstrating and advocating.

The concept of 'corporate advertising' focuses the subject of image too narrowly. Since all communications are seen as contributing to the corporate image, no one method or audience is more or less important than the others.

---

[8]*Understanding Media,* Marshall H. McLuhan, Bantam Books, New York, 1967.

Bearing this in mind, we're going to examine in the following chapters a number of corporations and the variety of missions they have assigned to image advertising. Although our efforts will be concentrated on media advertising, we will also cover, where appropriate, the many other forms of communications working in conjunction with an ad campaign. The programs we review may be far apart in objective and creative style, but they all have been successful in meeting their goals.

CHAPTER TWO

Establishing Favorable Market Position:
Building Public Awareness and Acceptance

■ "How do you give a single, believable personality to a highly diversified bank?"

"We set out to overcome a major corporate inferiority complex."

"Could image advertising help create preference for a low-interest, parity product?"

"Clearly our job was to develop an inviting, convincing national image."

"It was time to change our image from a stuffy commercial bank to an innovative, up-to-date investment bank."

"The public, including the media, didn't know who we were. They thought we were something we used to be. We had to change that."

Above are six disparate objectives for corporate image advertising, but all begin with the same mission: to establish more favorable market position. In each case the advertiser involved wished to raise the level of the company's public's awareness and increase acceptance for company products/services.

They understood that product advertising alone is often not sufficient to market effectively. When a company has a good image, the public will assume more readily that it produces good products and will be likely to pay more for those products. This holds true regardless of the target audience, whether it be the general consuming public, a vertical business market, the financial community, or government leaders.

Image advertising prepares your target publics for your point of view and products. It says to the customer: "You know who we are. You know what we stand for. You know you can trust us. You know you can trust our products. Let's do business."

Chemical Bank Seeks Unique Personality

In 1984 when Walter Shipley became Chairman of New York's Chemical Bank, he soon recognized that the bank was not projecting itself as clearly as it should to certain key audiences. The bank had a very broad customer base ranging from Fortune 500s through the middle market and the consumer market. But although it had a reasonably active and successful consumer advertising program, featuring basic consumer banking products, there was nothing to communicate the quality and the personality of the institution.

Shipley envisioned a corporate advertising campaign as only one of several marketing tools to be employed by the bank. These would include a much more active public speaking program for leading bank executives and more aggressive press relations.

There was also dissatisfaction with a prior, short-lived corporate campaign that Chemical Bank had run in 1982–83. The campaign had been so general and unspecific that it had no character to it. Almost any bank could have put its logo on those ads. Obviously Chemical needed its own unique personality.

Says Charles G. Salmans, senior vice president for Chemical Bank's corporate communications Department:

> The process of mounting a corporate campaign is a lengthy one. At least it took us about two years to get our program under way. First there was a long search for an agency we felt could work with us effectively in producing image ads. Then there were many interviews with bank officers, conducted by myself and agency executives, in an effort to determine how we were approaching our many various publics and just what image we should project.

How do you give a single personality to a bank as highly diversified as Chemical, reaching out to just about every possible customer constituency? And then how do you make that personality seem real and believable?

SPEAK OUT ON RELEVANT ISSUES

Chemical finally decided on an idea submitted by their newly selected corporate advertising agency: Lord, Geller, Federico, Einstein. The suggested campaign would convey a sense of knowledge of current banking world events by identifying some of the major issues that affect the banking system in general, Chemical Bank as an institution, and, most importantly, the bank's various customers.

Through speaking out on relevant issues, the bank felt it would be communicating to its publics—either directly or indirectly—such characteristics as managerial astuteness and the ability to think problems through, along with a sense of institutional direction and personality.

MAINTAIN A CONSISTENT, CONTINUING IMAGE

Salmans adds:

> In contrast to a lot of product advertising which needs to be very tactical to meet or even anticipate what a competitor might do, image advertising is a slow build. One of the mistakes I see being made by many institutions is their impulsive chopping and changing. The advertiser becomes bored with his own ads even before the marketplace does, and consequently changes something worthwhile into something else. He may even stop image advertising altogether.
>
> You've got to keep measuring the response to what you're doing. If you find that your program is reasonably on track, you must make sure that your campaign evolves . . . that you have a sense of continuity. The image that your target audience perceives in 1990 or 1991 should clearly relate to the image advertising they saw in 1987 or 1988.

Chemical Bank puts its money where its mouth is. Before launching their image advertising in 1986, it conducted a zero benchmark corporate image study. This was followed by more research, and there is another study in the planning stages as of this writing.

Initial research indicated that a couple of major bank failures, or near failures, were very much on the public mind at that time. Continental Illinois had had to be bailed out by the federal government, and both Mellon Bank and Bank of America had come close to the brink. Chemical's first ad tackled this subject head-on. The visual was a very overbuilt, very neon-cluttered highway, showing all of the ugliness of rapid, uncontrolled growth. The headline read:

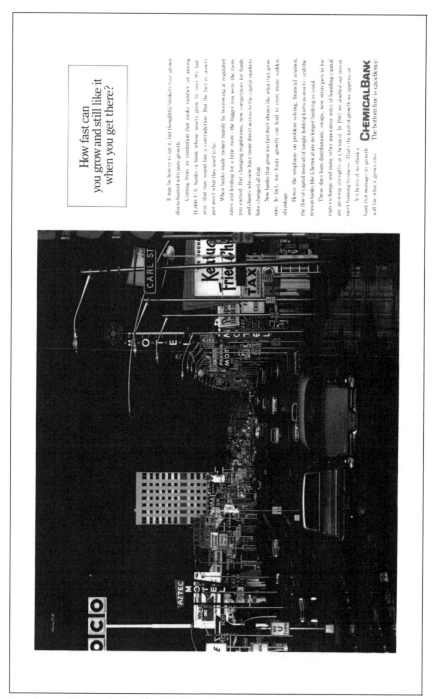

Reprinted with permission. © 1986 Chemical Bank.

Reprinted with permission. © 1987 Chemical Bank.

"How fast can you grow and still like it when you get there?" Copy talked about the question of banks, unlike other institutions, having to manage their growth, and how important this is to customers, employees, and shareholders alike.

Another ad, in a similar vein, dug into the difficult subject of credit culture. With some banks going belly-up under the pressure of too many bad decisions, thinking bankers and corporate customers appreciate the value of a banker who is not only a good salesperson but also understands how to make sound credit judgments. The visual for this particular ad was a little white mouse perched on a piece of cheese, and the headline read: "How do you stick to your credit culture when temptation's right under your nose?" Copy focuses on the balanced role the banker must play in today's broader, more fiercely competitive marketplace. It makes the point that credit culture is as much an *attitude* as it is a set of rules . . . that Chemical Bank has a willingness to look a little deeper into a deal, work a little harder with a business or individual. The ad, and all others in the campaign, signs off with the tag line, "The bottom line is excellence," reflecting Chemical's commitment to excellence in everything they elect to do . . . their custom of dealing with important issues in a thoughtful, disciplined, and well-managed way.

Believing in consistency, the bank has no immediate plans to change a successful message and format. In mid-1987, one and a half years after the start of the campaign, Chemical added to their subject list the whole question of regulatory and legislative reform. This move widened the campaign's horizons but in no way altered its premise.

Three Basic Principles

Salmans concludes:

> We attack subjects that get to the heart of the commercial banking business . . . subjects that sort out successful banks from the unsuccessful. By approaching these issues squarely, we express our own philosophy and encourage people to understand Chemical's personality as an institution.

The technique works. Target audiences not only notice but read the Chemical advertising. The bank has purchased Starch Reports thirteen times, with their ad achieving "Best Read" in the financial category twelve times out of thirteen. The ads are also considered an important internal morale booster, with feedback from employees being very favorable. It has even been said that the image campaign helps create a valuable sense of employee "ownership."

Why does it work? For one thing, Chemical's advertising follows three basic principles of successful image programs:

1. The bank understands the direction it must take to establish its quality and personality with many different audiences;

2. The ads themselves are well written with timely, provocative headlines; they feature dramatic color photography and utilize dominant space in appropriate media;

3. Chemical recognizes the tremendous value to image projection of consistency and continuity.

Of course, as might be expected, Chemical's chairman is very much involved with the image campaign, and those who work on the ads—both at the bank and at the agency—regard his support and input as vital to the advertising's success.

The Wausau Story

Consistency is not exclusively a Chemical Bank concept. Listen to Robert W. Gunderson, vice president for advertising at Wausau Insurance Companies.

> Consistency has always been a big thing with me in my nearly forty years of doing this advertising—consistency in message and consistency in media selection.
>
> But consistency doesn't have to mean sameness. We've tried to keep our ad designs contemporary and inviting, our copy short and to the point, and our commercials lighthearted. No advertiser, regardless of the expenditure, can purchase the right to bore people.

In January 1954, a few million readers opened their *Time* magazines and found an ad featuring a small-town railroad depot at dusk, with the headline: "How come one of the world's most important insurance companies is located in Wausau, Wisconsin?" They were seeing for the very first time an example of what was to become the American advertising classic known as "The Wausau Story." They were also being introduced to the Wausau depot, which would become one of the more unique and recognizable corporate trademarks. In effect they were witnessing a bold attempt—and in time a highly successful one—to cure a major corporate inferiority complex!

Today, 35 years later, Wausau's must be the best-known depot in the world, with the possible exception of Grand Central Station. And studies show that Wausau's commercials on "60 Minutes" are consistently better remembered

How come one of the world's most important
insurance companies is located in Wausau, Wisconsin?

The fishing's good near Wausau. It's only a stone's throw to where the deer run. Once in a while, they say, a lynx comes down from the north.

And it's the home of one of the world's most important insurance companies.

How come?

This was lumber country once. And lumbering was a hazardous business. 43 years ago a group of lumbermen joined together to pay the claims of injured sawmill workers under Wisconsin's new workmen's compensation law. The group came to be called The Employers Mutuals of Wausau.

Wausau is no longer lumber country. But Employers Mutuals has stayed. So have the men who guided the company from the very beginning.

How come?

Because they knew that something good had grown up there. A certain way of doing business that was good. An almost *personal* character. A fairness that bent over backward rather than forward. Policyholders and their employees kept saying that Employers Mutuals were "good people to do business with."

There was a "Wausau personality" about us that people seemed to like and we didn't

want to lose. We're a large company today. We write all types of casualty and fire insurance, and are one of the very largest in workmen's compensation. We have two reputations, born and raised in Wausau, that we aim to hold. One is unexcelled service on claims. The other is an accident prevention program that means lower costs to policyholders.

We're still "Wausau." But today there are offices of Employers Mutuals of Wausau in 89 cities. "A little bit of Wausau on the sidewalks of New York." And we're still good people to do business with.

Employers Mutuals *of* Wausau   "Good people to do business with"

Courtesy of Wausau Insurance Companies.

than those of much larger advertisers. It's been a long time since the Wausau image took a backseat to anyone's.

TURNING A PERCEIVED DISADVANTAGE INTO AN ASSET

How did such a memorable and long-running ad campaign get its start? It was shortly after World War II, and Wausau was reaching out for national markets. They had run occasional ads in *Time* and a few other national publications, and had done a little radio, but by their own admission, it was "pretty forgettable stuff."

In June 1953, the company retained J. Walter Thompson to create a more comprehensive and competitive campaign. After a thorough study of Wausau, its people, policyholders, former customers, and prospects, Thompson concluded that the company was suffering from a corporate inferiority complex— the result of being located in the North Woods instead of a big financial center.

Gunderson comments: "Thompson felt we could turn the perceived disadvantage of our small-town beginnings into an asset. We could talk about accepted values of small-town America, such as home-town neighborliness and personal concern. Another asset we had was the very name of our hometown. Wausau was an unusual place name (in the Chippewa tongue it means "far-away place"), and we alone could lay claim to it."

The very first advertising objective read: "To set Wausau apart from all other companies and create a strong identity and personality of our own." The particular image to be created was one of "size large enough to handle any risk." Among the target audiences selected were medium to large corporations, and their risk managers, financial officers, CEOs, senior vice presidents, and board members.

While the strategy for the new campaign was being formulated, Everett McNear, a prominent commercial artist, was hired to do an illustration for the first ad. What McNear created has earned its place as a classic in corporate identity—the Wausau depot. Although the depot did not immediately become Wausau's trademark, it was soon apparent that the illustration had captivated a lot of readers. It actually got fan mail, and hundreds of frameable prints were mailed out.

EVOLUTION OF THE CAMPAIGN

For the first couple of years all the ads were done in Wausau. A succession of prominent people were brought to town, shown around, and interviewed as to their impressions of Wausau—the community and the company. These were highly credible spokesmen, like George Romney, president of American Motors, and Don Douglas of Douglas Aircraft. The insights they offered made for extremely readable and effective advertising.

After establishing the Wausau identity, the campaign went "on the road" to cities where the company had regional offices. The resulting series of ads carried headlines like: "A Little Bit of Wausau on the Sidewalks of New York"; "A Little Bit of Wausau Deep in the Heart of Texas"; and "A Little Bit of Wausau in Sunny California."

With the theme firmly established, Wausau moved to the case study format they still use. Ads are low-key but sales supportive. Satisfied policyholders talk about the benefits of their relationship with the company, but instead of traditional accident and catastrophe stories ads accent the positive. They show how to prevent the business catastrophe from happening and discuss the many ways Wausau can be a valuable resource for policyholders.

Ads feature eye-catching color photography and neatly pointed headlines. For Magnetek, for example, there's a beautiful nighttime shot of New York's Trade Center with the Statue of Liberty in the foreground. The headline reads: "A company whose products help light entire cities has a power source in Wausau."

An ad featuring Great Northern Nekoosa Corporation is illustrated by a three-dimensional map of North America, constructed from papers made by Nekoosa Papers, Inc., and with the headline: "How Wausau helps great Northern Nekoosa spread out across the country."

Both ads are shown here. So, too, is one of the few ads in the series that deviates from the format. This is Wausau's thirty-fifth anniversary ad, appearing in January 1989. Its railroad station graphic, with the ghost images of life around a turn-of-the-century depot, is reminiscent of the very first ad's depot artwork. The headline is perfectly matched to the art: "The trains are gone now. And their sounds are just an echo in the mind."

Much of the language in this ad comes from ads and commercials of years past. It is an excellent example of how a campaign can derive strength from those who touched it in the past.

An Untested TV Program Called "60 Minutes"

When the popular weekly magazine *The Saturday Evening Post* died, Wausau looked for a way to replace its important 6.5 million circulation. They took a chance on a new, untested TV program called "60 Minutes." It was a decision based on instinct and pure faith.

The program aired originally without too much success on Saturday evenings. It moved to Thursday, and finally to Sunday. There it found its proper niche and today is watched faithfully by more than 25 million people.

A company whose products help light entire cities has a power source in Wausau.

MagneTek has electrical equipment in office buildings and factories across the country. They have products in an estimated 9 out of every 10 households. And they have their business insurance in Wausau.

"We needed an insurer who could step in and supply us with strong loss control support," says Dennis G. Berndt, Director of Insurance and Risk Management for the Los Angeles-based company.

"Wausau has worked closely with our people: implementing training programs, injury avoidance programs and ergonomic surveys. Together we've been able to lower losses substantially."

Controlling losses and the resulting insurance costs takes energy and experience. It takes the business insurance experts from Wausau, and a committed policyholder like MagneTek.

WAUSAU INSURANCE

Wausau Insurance Companies, 2000 Westwood Drive, Wausau, Wisconsin 54401 Telephone (715) 845-5211 A Member of the Nationwide® Group.

10-652-435   1188

Courtesy of Wausau Insurance Companies.

Great Northern Nekoosa Corporation of Stamford, Connecticut, is a major and fast-growing producer of pulp and paper. They rely on the coordinated efforts of our network of regional offices to cover 12,000 of their employees in 120 locations.

"Wausau never fails to meet our insurance needs, and our needs change from day to day," says GNN Executive Vice President Jim Crump. "Right now, we're in the process of linking our company directly to Wausau's computer, so we can analyze any situation immediately."

American businesses choose Wausau because we give them more than insurance. We give them the best service in the business. And companies like Great Northern Nekoosa don't even mind saying so, on paper.

Wausau Insurance Companies.   2000 Westwood Drive, Wausau, Wisconsin 54401   Telephone (715) 845-5211   A Member of the Nationwide Group

10-652-423   688

Courtesy of Wausau Insurance Companies.

The trains are gone now.
And their sounds are just an echo in the mind.

But this little depot keeps on working, reminding you and us that business insurance ought to work for a living. Getting your money's worth ought not be just a thing of the past.

We have two reputations, born and raised in Wausau and exported to our offices throughout America: One is exceptional and consistent claim service - and the other is proven effective loss control services that can help lower costs for policyholders.

Wherever America does business, Wausau's there - with business insurance professionals in 140 cities.

WAUSAU INSURANCE

Wausau Insurance Companies, 2000 Westwood Drive, Wausau, Wisconsin 54401 Telephone (715) 845-5211 A Member of the Nationwide® Group

10 652 439   189

Courtesy of Wausau Insurance Companies.

Notes Gunderson:

We're the only advertiser that has been with them continuously since the early days when they were struggling to get started. "60 Minutes" has been our flagship on TV.

Of course we continue to study and research our audience—those people who influence the business insurance buying decision. It's an upscale but ever-changing universe. They are better-educated, fact-oriented people. That's the reason we like news magazines and TV news programming. This kind of media attracts people with inquiring minds.

Peripheral Benefits

Not only has the Wausau advertising created and maintained the desired corporate image over the years, but it has also been an invaluable sales tool. Thousands and thousands of reprints are used by the salespeople each year as convincing "proof sources" of the company's effective service. And more than one employee claims that it was a Wausau ad that first attracted them to the company.

Not the least of its benefits is the salutary effect the campaign has had on the town of Wausau itself. Almost every resident who travels has a story about favorable comments in faraway places when it became known that they were from Wausau, the real "faraway place." This particular image advertising is, perhaps, the quintessential community relations program.

The Wausau story goes on, still quietly persuading prospects that the company is "good people to do business with." The campaign may have been refined from time to time, but thematically it's the same as it was when it started—building awareness and acceptance by telling stories of satisfied Wausau customers.

The Qualities of Corporate Character

To build and maintain such a favorable image, Wausau knew that it needed to communicate the vital statistics of its corporate character. So does any other company that looks to improve its public image and gain acceptance as a leader in the marketplace. They need to articulate clearly just who they are and what they do . . . corporate philosophy and purpose . . . quality of management . . . a sense of responsibility to peers, stockholders, the public . . . plans for the future . . . and prospects for growth.

Essential qualities of successful corporate campaigns generally include:

1. *Simplicity:* The best corporate campaigns do not seek to be all things to all people. Rather they focus on a single important idea that can be developed over time and presented in a variety of creative executions.

2. *Uniqueness.* The theme a company selects must differentiate it from competitors. For example, corporate advertising in the high-technology area is inundated with claims of proficiency and innovation.

3. *Appropriateness.* Good corporate advertising brings attention to a company; great corporate advertising brings attention to qualities that further corporate objectives.

4. *Relevance.* The best corporate campaigns hit home with their target audiences.

5. *Foresight.* A key objective of image advertising is to reach people before they formulate negative opinions. This way, when an intelligent, persuasive ad campaign is implemented, the public can be convinced that your view is correct (or at least see the value of your argument.)

6. *Continuity.* Continuity is the key to successful corporate advertising. Corporate advertising requires high visibility for the long term.

7. *Credibility.* A corporate campaign, no matter how well planned or well funded it may be, cannot succeed if its claims do not match reality.[1]

Under the Travelers Red Umbrella

Another major insurance company that relies on image advertising to build awareness and acceptance is The Travelers Corporation, although their objectives are vastly different from Wausau's.

Once Travelers simply supplied lines of insurance, but with deregulation they added health maintenance and preferred-provider organizations. They also began to underwrite mortgages and offer IRAs and mutual funds. Practically overnight Travelers became a full-fledged financial services company, but the general public still didn't realize it.

"There was a lack of awareness of who we were," says one corporate spokesman. Increasingly, top management was beginning to see, he explains, "that corporate advertising gives you a foundation to build upon *when* you want to, *if* you want to—so that later you can leverage the corporate image instead of having to build up the image of the product alone."

---

[1]Condensed from *Grey Matter,* reprinted courtesy of Grey Advertising, Inc.

Starting in 1985, The Travelers began featuring their famous red umbrella symbol in a series of ads that asked: "Have you looked under the umbrella lately?" By 1987 the umbrella was starring in focus ads that highlighted information on the company's specific divisions. Unaided advertising awareness went up by 133 percent. "Let's face it," says the spokesman, "it's a war out there. Whether you're a brokerage house, an insurance company, or a bank, you're all going after the same discretionary dollar."[2]

The "crash" of October 19, 1987, shook a lot of people up and changed some traditional ways of thinking. Market research, both of a quantitative and qualitative nature, was done to determine current wants and needs of the consumer and the businessperson in terms of insurance and investment strategies. Findings indicated that the desire to be financially secure and maintain status quo was paramount, and that insurance companies were considered the cornerstone of an investment portfolio.

Timing couldn't have been better to develop the corporate image campaign further.

CREATING PREFERENCE FOR A PARITY PRODUCT

The spokesman continues:

> We are in a low-interest category, offering a parity product with a lot of other insurance companies. The way to set ourselves apart may not be so much by product differences as by the way in which our company is perceived. The public's increased desire for financial security gave us the ideal focal point for new image advertising.
>
> Naturally the campaign was designed to reinforce our reputation as a preeminent supplier of insurance and financial services. It would also establish that The Travelers' real job is to manage uncertainty, and that the product we offer isn't so much insurance or investments but rather financial peace of mind.

Ads feature dramatic color photography, short copy, and headlines which play decidedly to this craving for financial security.

A typical consumer ad shows a skier soaring high over a snowy mountain scene, with the headline: "Financial serenity: the ability to soar above worry and insecurity."

---

[2]"Rain Gear," Kristin Nord, *Public Relations Journal,* September 1987.

In like manner, the first new ad aimed at the business community is headed: "Our client list includes 50% of the Fortune 500. The bottom line is your financial peace of mind."

The artwork is a delineation of the highly recognizable Travelers Umbrella, encompassing a color photograph of the New York skyline and World Trade Center. Both consumer and business ads feature the Red Umbrella in the logo, along with the tag line "You're better off under the Umbrella."

At this writing it's much too early to verify how well this image advertising is working. In-depth developmental research, however, during the campaign's conceptual stages, seems to point to ultimate success. A variety of groups, representing Travelers' different target audiences, were studied, and their reaction to the proposed advertising was excellent. Continued testing is part of the plan.

The spokesman concludes:

> The important thing was to be sure the campaign had enough "noise level" to break through the clutter of all the other advertising. First we had to figure exactly what that noise level is. We closely monitored 23 key competitors and 6 core competitors in terms of their spending levels.
>
> We used that evaluation to determine the share of voice figures that we should maintain and share of voice against an average market share. We try to keep our efforts at least at this level. Anything less and we would start to suffer.

Promoting a Vibrant Atmosphere

Corporations aren't the only beneficiaries of improved awareness. A telephone study for the Greater Raleigh Chamber of Commerce of 250 corporate executives in the Northeast and Midwest showed that Raleigh was known for tobacco but not much else. This finding was supported by an economic strategic study in the mid-1980s by the Arthur D. Little Company. In effect it said: "The state of North Carolina is known and the 'Research Triangle' (Raleigh-Durham-Chapel Hill) is known, but Raleigh itself isn't. You need to develop a national image for Raleigh." Jerry Brown, the Chamber's former vice president, puts it this way: "People who were looking for the right place to live and do business needed to look at the vitality, energy, and momentum of Raleigh. We hoped to bring new and expanding companies to the Raleigh area by emphasizing our special charged atmosphere."

"COME SEIZE THE FUTURE"

The Chamber's advertising budget did not allow for a massive campaign of dominant-space, color ads in a long list of publications. Ads were black-and-white, and, in addition to spreads and single pages, fractional units were used to provide continuity. Media was pretty much limited to *Industrial Week, Business Week,* and the *Wall Street Journal.*

What the campaign may have lacked in amplitude it made up for in creative quality. Major ads, with headlines such as "One thing about movers and shakers. They move to where they can shake," helped build awareness of greater Raleigh's bright future, and conveyed an image of excitement and growth. Ads featured leading executives whose companies have settled in Raleigh, a technique suggestive of the "satisfied customer" format of Wausau.

To add frequency to the campaign, fractional pages (see illustrations), relying almost solely on headlines, focused on specific and relevant facts about Raleigh's industrial and business expansion.

All the ads, full-size and fractional, were signed with the theme line: "Raleigh. Come Seize The Future," pointing to the new spirit, energy, and potential of greater Raleigh.

DEVELOP A NEW DIRECTION

Ads included a private phone line to Jerry Brown at the Raleigh Chamber of Commerce, a mailing address, and an occasional coupon. Response, especially in the first year or so of the campaign, was substantial. Since the campaign broke in late 1986, over 50 corporations have either moved into Raleigh or have expanded existing businesses, with a local investment of more than $700 million.

Equally pertinent, population growth in Raleigh has soared to an annual rate of 5.5 percent, putting the city among the top 10 in the nation. For comparison's sake, the state of North Carolina is growing at a rate of only 1.2 percent per year.

Respondents to the image campaign were carefully evaluated. More than two-thirds of these contacts came from the Northeast. In addition, 50 percent of those who have moved to Raleigh in the past 10 years came from the Northeast.

As a result Raleigh will soon be shifting its advertising emphasis. A new campaign, which was scheduled for late 1989, aims more at target audiences in New Jersey, New York (especially New York City and Long Island), and Fairfield County, Connecticut. Appropriate local and regional media will be used.

One Thing About Movers And Shakers. They Move To Where They Can Shake.

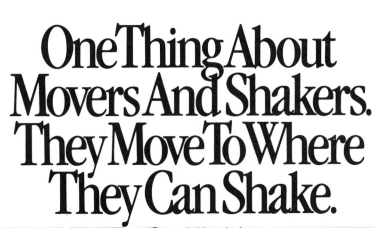

Suzanne Troxler Babcock, Vice President Administration
Troxler Laboratories, Inc.
World's Leading Manufacturer Of Nuclear Road Gauges.

James H. Maynard, Chief Executive Officer
Golden Corral Corporation
Nation's Largest Operator Of Family Steakhouses With 466 Restaurants.

Andy Dembicks, Founder And President
Southern Case, Inc.
World's Largest Manufacturer Of Specialty Cases.

Some places have a special way of inspiring accomplishment.
There's an energy, a spirit, that encourages great things. And it's what's drawing the vital, forward-thinking people of our time to one place in particular. Raleigh, North Carolina.

Because in Raleigh, you'll find a city built by an excitement, not an establishment. A city whose spirit gives you the room to surge ahead. And the right to stir things up. And that, my friend, is a spirit that a lot of cities have lost. And one that a lot of cities never really had.

So when you're ready to make your move, make it Raleigh. We'll give you all the room you need to shake. And the solid ground to do it on.

Contact Jerry Brown. Chamber of Commerce, PO Box 2978, Raleigh, NC 27602, 919-833-9400

Raleigh
Come Seize The Future.

Courtesy of Raleigh Chamber of Commerce.

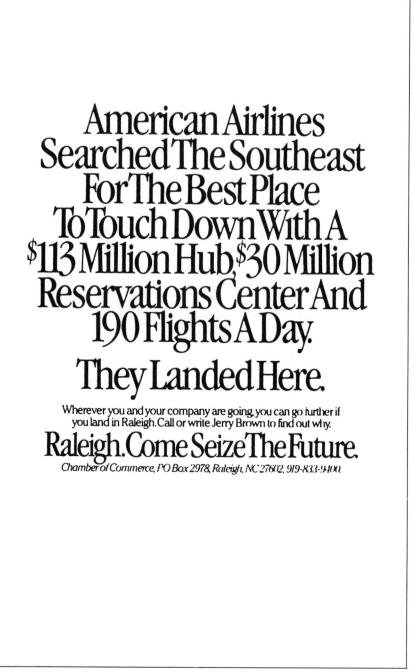

Courtesy of Raleigh Chamber of Commerce.

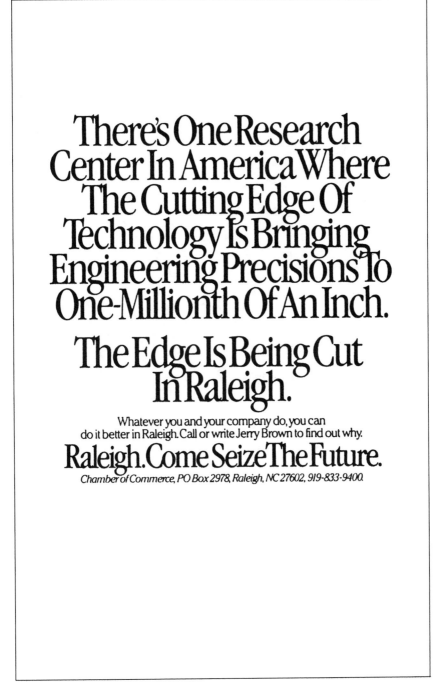

Courtesy of Raleigh Chamber of Commerce.

Courtesy of Raleigh Chamber of Commerce.

Although the target may now be more focused, the objective is still the same: to establish favorable market position among peer and competing areas and "sell Greater Raleigh as a great place to live and work."

Always Start with Research

Casey Stengel is reputed to have said: "If you don't know where you are, you may not be there." He couldn't have described the purpose of image research any better. A company should always know where its corporate image is—and where it's going.

Yankelovich Clancy Shulman, noted market research consultants, put it this way: "Intelligence. It's what helps us make the right business decisions that lead to one thing: more successes with fewer failures . . . A company learns what it needs to know about itself and its markets in order to set objectives it can achieve successfully."[3]

And Harry O'Neill of Opinion Research Corporation has this to say: "Regardless of how complex the genesis of a corporate image, or how true or how false it may be, behavior is related to the image. Companies are affected, for better or worse, by their images. Thus there is indeed value in knowing as much about your image as possible from as many publics as you deem important to the well being of your company."[4]

We have seen already in this chapter how four advertisers have used research, in one form or another, to determine their need for image advertising and/or measure results. These companies are certainly not exceptions. Today almost any corporation that is serious about having an image program employs research.

In 1980, of the nation's largest 500 industrial corporations, almost half—244—opted for such programs. The top 20 companies in the oil industry were all image researchers, as well as three-quarters of the companies in the aerospace industry. With each succeeding year new numbers of well-known corporations jump on the image research bandwagon.

---

[3]Reprinted from a corporate brochure "Marketing Intelligence," Yankelovich Clancy Shulman, 1987.

[4]"The Research Behind a Corporate Campaign," Harry O'Neill, reprinted from *Crosscurrents*, Vol. 7, 1978.

Morgan's Strong but Brief Beginning

One advertiser that got aboard that bandwagon some time ago was Morgan Guaranty Trust Company (now signing its ads J.P. Morgan). In the early 1960s, there began to be a nagging suspicion in the minds of bank management that perhaps Morgan might need some sort of corporate advertising program. Competitors were already using advertising to establish and maintain image.

A key adviser, David Ogilvy—whose Ogilvy & Mather advertising agency had been started a few years earlier with the help of a Morgan loan—disagreed, interestingly enough. He had counseled for some time that Morgan stood out from the pack by *not* advertising.

To help illumine the debate, the Roper Organization was called in to study a cross-section of the Morgan audience of corporate and financial officers to see how well the bank compared. Results were shocking. Clearly the bank did not stand out very well. It was a blurry image at best, one of a stuffy bank with dark paneled walls and thick carpets . . . of bankers who wore black ties and white shirts. All in all, a bank without much flair . . . not very innovative. Worst of all, while management thought Morgan unique in primarily serving corporate customers, its market didn't perceive this at all.

It was obvious that it was high time to raise awareness as to what Morgan stood for. Principles were established that, to large extent, J.P. Morgan followed for more than 15 years. Ads in the campaign had headlines that said something about Morgan's business philosophy and capabilities. Copy was long but readable and compelling. (Some of the first ads were written by David Ogilvy.)

Dominant space was bought, but in deference to budget limitations, magazine ads were in black and white. Leading business magazines of the day were used, along with the *New York Herald-Tribune,* the *New York Times,* and the *Wall Street Journal.* In each was displayed a small photo of Morgan's famous entrance at 23 Wall Street.

The campaign was launched in 1964, after four years of deliberation and preparation. This was not a major impact program. It was effective, however, creating attention because it was startling to see staid old Morgan actually talk about itself in print. Once upon a time they had paid people to keep the Morgan name out of the papers.

That first campaign lasted two years. A massive credit crunch in 1966 brought a temporary end to Morgan's image efforts. The bank was now getting more loan requests than it wanted or could handle. Advertising had to go.

TIE ADS TOGETHER WITH A TAG LINE

When it began again in 1968, credit problems now history, the messages still stressed Morgan's corporate banking services, and now were signed, "Morgan Guaranty—the corporate bank."

Late in 1969, however, a conflict emerged with another Ogilvy client, and Morgan began a search for a new agency. A small and relatively unknown shop, Friedlich, Fearon & Strohmeier, won the assignment with a well-thought-out creative presentation. Included was a basic theme: "Consider Morgan Guaranty." Used in all headlines, regardless of products featured, the line tied all ads together for the next eight years. All that time, the signature remained: "Morgan Guaranty—the corporate bank."

"We were determined to be consistent," remembers Bruce Roberts, Morgan vice president and former advertising director. "We felt—and still feel—that consistency adds to the effectiveness of any image program. But to be able to maintain consistency you've got to start somewhere. We began with four basic objectives and then decided on several tactics to reach our goals. Applying these strategies consistently over the years has paid off for us in an advertising program that we believe has been successful in meeting our objectives. A lot of this is basic, but it's surprising how often advertisers lose sight of basics."

Morgan's first goal was to make Morgan Guaranty better known as a premier, worldwide corporate bank. Second, they wanted to increase market awareness of their more profit-promising services. They also wanted to build image and show that Morgan's real cutting edge was people—extremely competent and experienced banking specialists. Fourth, management understood and accepted that any real payoff on the campaign would be long-range rather than short.

Several key tactics were developed by the bank and their agency; some are still basic to Morgan advertising today:

1. Descriptive copy making a distinct point about a single service.

2. The recurring theme, "Consider Morgan Guaranty," as part of every headline to link the different ads in the campaign.

3. A photograph of actual Morgan bankers at work.

4. The use of color, for extra visibility and impact.

5. Consistent use of the photo of the bank's entrance at 23 Wall Street.

6. The purchase of dominant space.

7. The use of dominant media.

8. Overseas, the use of the language of the country in which the ad appears.

9. A consistency of graphics to give Morgan Guaranty ads anywhere in the world a similarity of look.

Taking the Chill Off

Bruce Roberts notes:

> We had, like many banks, a reputation for being cold. The agency recommendation was "You've got to warm up the bank!" It was their suggestion that the ads show our people in interesting work situations. This may not sound particularly daring now, but in 1970 no other bank was doing it. Top management bought the concept, and we began running color ads that featured our officers in action—on the way to meetings, in conference, working in shirtsleeves, with computers.
>
> Over the following years, scores of this kind of ad were developed. We did studies every two or three years to see how well they were received. Research showed that the ads were doing their job very well indeed, and the cumulative effect was especially impressive.

THE EVOLUTION OF A NAME

From time to time Morgan was faced with an additional image question. Changing circumstances necessitated changes in their marketing name.

Following the merger in 1959 of the old J.P. Morgan & Co. and Guaranty Trust Company, the bank adopted the name Morgan Guaranty Trust Company, and that's how the first ads were signed. As we have seen, it later changed its signature to "Morgan Guaranty—the corporate bank." Then when Morgan began mounting a major effort in private banking, they felt they were being hurt by their strong image as a corporate bank. So they dropped "the corporate bank" and for a short time used simply Morgan Guaranty Trust Company.

In the late seventies, learning from research and other feedback that they were commonly referred to as The Morgan Bank, the bank changed to that as a quicker, cleaner way of getting their name across. Then too, the campaign had become international in scope, with ads in a wide variety of foreign languages, and The Morgan Bank translated far better than did Morgan Guaranty Trust Company. The Morgan Bank was its marketing name for nine years.

BACK TO ROOTS

The whole financial services industry and marketplace began to change radically in the 1980s. It was evident that Morgan needed to get back into some of the businesses with which they had formerly served large corporations. With the tremendous growth of commercial paper, target customers could now lend to each other and no longer needed to come to Morgan for loans. They did, however, need bond issues, foreign exchange, advice on mergers and acquisitions, and the like—many services not normally associated with a commercial bank.

These were the investment banking services for which the old J.P. Morgan & Co. had been famous. Regulatory changes were now breaking down some of the walls between investment banking and commercial banking. With this in mind, many of the senior officers felt they should no longer call themselves a bank. It seemed natural to change the bank's name again—this time going back to the roots of J.P. Morgan. (J.P. Morgan & Co. had been resurrected as the name of the holding company established in 1969, with Morgan Guaranty Trust Company as its principal subsidiary.)

More Identity Problems

But before deciding to emphasize a new name, the bank needed to address several problems. First, with Morgan's proposed direction as an investment bank, the old commercial banking heritage would have to be tempered and changed. The new perception had to be that The Morgan Bank was a major player in corporate finance and advisory services, securities sales and trading, and so forth. The problem was how to make Morgan seem less like a commercial bank, an outfit that knows how to lend money and handle payrolls, and more like an investment bank; that is, a competitive, marketwise institution able to move quickly and offer quality advice across a broad financial services spectrum.

Then too, the recent deregulation of American banks had encouraged Morgan to create a number of subsidiaries. Many took a J.P. Morgan name because they were holding company subsidiaries rather than commercial banking subsidiaries. The Morgan Bank ended up doing business alongside J.P. Morgan Investment Management, J.P. Morgan Securities, J.P. Morgan whatever. The result was total confusion.

Added to this was the wave of violence in Europe in the mid-1980s. Much of this was directed at the officers of major multi-national corporations doing business there. Bank management now had real concern over the use of photos of their officers in advertising. The continuing use of these pictures, which had become something of a hallmark, could be an undue security risk for their staff. Although the bank might change or even discontinue advertising in Europe, they recognized that the terrorism could spread. It was obvious that Morgan could no longer employ the old format everywhere. It was time to do something else.

The fact was that after 17 years of complete consistency, Morgan's ads were instantly recognizable no matter what name they used. The ads said "commercial bank" no matter what the subject. The format had become totally associated with The Morgan Bank—a commercial bank. In order to break that association and represent the bank to potential customers, Morgan needed to change not only its name but also the look of its advertising.

SETTING THE COURSE

The bank conducted an in-depth, one-on-one study of senior officers to verify whether they really felt that their commercial banking image had to be modified, and if they agreed, what the bank should be called and what attributes needed to be conveyed with the new name.

The agency also did an external study for Morgan to identify the "hot buttons" which would cause a CEO or CFO to consider the bank as a valuable addition to his or her roster of advisers. Research showed that a very high premium was placed on the integrity and ethical character of financial institutions. This was one area where Morgan scored well ahead of the rest of the field.

In the spring of 1987 the bank approved *J. P. Morgan* as its worldwide marketing name and adopted *integrity* and *brainpower* as the critical positioning elements for Morgan advertising. They remain so today.

A NEW LOOK BUT THE SAME PRINCIPLES

The new look no longer shows bank officers in action around the world, and copy is now decidedly shorter. Ads focus dramatically on the bank's abilities in corporate finance, advisory, and capital markets services. As can be seen in the illustrations they signal strongly that Morgan changes as financial markets change, but still does business on the same sound principles and ethics as before. As the headline for the very first of the new ads proclaims: "The techniques change. The principles don't."

Subsequent ads would highlight such bank characteristics as *objectivity, confidentiality,* and *innovativeness,* as well as develop the theme of Morgan's unique blend of global experience and capabilities.

These ads show the advantages of doing business with Morgan; they communicate the differences between Morgan and other banks; and they show how Morgan's basic principles and way of doing business offer benefits to clients.

"The techniques change. The principles don't."

Combining capital strength with financing, advisory, trading, and investment skills throughout the world, J.P. Morgan continues to innovate to serve our clients better. Yet the principles that guide us in today's integrated, technology-driven financial markets haven't changed in 150 years.

In everything we do the client's interests come first, a way of doing business that produces impartial, objective advice on any matter, however confidential. Many years ago J.P. Morgan himself said it best: "The client's belief in the integrity of our advice is our best possession."

Change linked to continuity: J.P. Morgan's new headquarters rise on Wall Street two blocks from where the firm has had its principal offices for more than a century.

JPMorgan

Courtesy of J. P. Morgan & Co. Incorporated.

As always, Morgan used research to be sure they were on the right track. They commissioned in-depth studies to measure ad effectiveness, focusing on readership and favorability. Results have been uniformly positive.

Stan Hironaka, who succeeded Roberts as vice president for advertising in 1988, concludes:

> We see a continuing need to build worldwide recognition of the J.P. Morgan name, and of the evolving nature of our services. Advertising is a primary way of achieving this. We look on it as an important long-term investment, not a short-term expense. Considering present international business conditions, we believe Morgan has a real opportunity, through continued effective advertising, to help further build our reputation for integrity, consistency, and excellence.

Westinghouse: The Best Unknown Company in America

Westinghouse is one of comparatively few companies that have had the same name for more than 100 years. A well-known name, too, but not a well-understood name. For too long, target publics—business executives, government officials, the financial world, even the media—have thought of Westinghouse in terms of refrigerators and light bulbs. Only recently have they begun to understand that the company has not been in those businesses for years . . . that Westinghouse is actually now a leader in such areas as financial services, broadcasting, electronics, environmental technologies, energy, and others.

In 1983, Westinghouse began a series of perception studies, identifying target audiences and establishing perceptions as to what the company is all about. Results clearly showed Westinghouse was associated with the past. Later research, completed in 1985, 1986, and 1987, corroborated the findings. The company was still thought to be in consumer appliances by 52 percent of customers and business leaders, 43 percent of investors, and a surprising 83 percent of the media.

In June 1989, in an effort to counteract this and introduce today's Westinghouse, the company launched an extensive campaign in leading business journals. Its objective was to enhance the value of Westinghouse to investors, employees, shareholders, and customers by increasing their understanding of the company and its future. Scheduled to run for three years, the campaign has the theme: "Westinghouse. The Best Unknown Company in America."

One of the first ads set the scene with a quote from John C. Marous, Chairman and CEO. "When a company has a name as well-known as Westinghouse,

This ad appears in The New York Times and the Washington Post, May 31, courtesy of the business publications shown in the above illustration.

Courtesy of Westinghouse.

Courtesy of Westinghouse.

people think they know what you do. People think we still make appliances. We haven't made them in 15 years. People think we still make light bulbs. We haven't made them in over six years . . . We're a company you should get to know better.''

The image campaign kicked off with 10 consecutive right hand pages in the *Wall Street Journal,* covering the many businesses Westinghouse is in today. Subsequently individual pages were run as separate ads. In the business magazines, the ads ran as spreads, each dramatized by top-quality color photography (see illustrations) and to-the-point headlines like: ''Over 100 million people tune us in every day'' and ''We're America's largest finance company providing capital exclusively to business.''

Bob Lukovics, director of corporate advertising, has this to add: ''In addition to our initial perception studies, we also looked at other companies, examining what they were doing, to help us establish realistic objectives. We felt that the ideal concept was that the better people knew you, the more they were going to like you. We still believe that, and although the campaign is not over, our tracking phone interviews encourage us that it is working.''

The Corporate Advertiser Has the Advantage

As a final word, a recent *Grey Matter* states:

> . . . in a study sponsored by *Time,* the research firm Yankelovich, Skelly and White found that companies that practice corporate advertising outscore nonpractitioners in literally every area examined.
>
> The corporate advertiser has the advantage in categories such as increased awareness; overall favorable impressions (such as job recommendations, stock investment, and agreement with corporate positions in controversies); and association with positive traits (such as high-quality products, innovativeness, good financial performance, competent management, and honesty).[5]

We have seen how several corporations have used image advertising to alter the perceptions of their publics and create a more realistic awareness of themselves in the marketplace. Reasons may have been different, but results were the same: better educated target audiences leading to greater understanding and acceptance of the company, its products and programs.

---

[5]*Grey Matter,* Vol. 54, Number 2, 1983, reprinted courtesy of Grey Advertising, Inc.

CHAPTER THREE

Redefining the Corporation:
Merger, Takeover, and Other Reasons for Name Change

■ Corporate image advertising, especially of the name change variety, goes hand in hand with the recent merger/acquisition craze. And we are seeing more and more of it. According to identity consultants Anspach Grossman Portugal, 1988 saw 1864 corporate name changes, with another 1600 in 1989.

A few of the recently renamed corporations include Navistar (formerly International Harvester), Primerica Corporation (from American Can), Trinova Corporation (it was Libbey-Owens-Ford), Unisys Corporation (created from the merger of Burroughs and Sperry), GTE (once upon a time the General Telephone and Electronics Corporation), and CSX (formed through the merger of Chessie System Railroads and Seaboard Coastline Industries). In each case some sort of image campaign was employed to announce the new name and redefine the corporation in terms of its revised organization and future direction.

Image in Corporate Takeovers

Image advertising has also become a critical marketing weapon in the power struggle against corporate takeovers. Douglas Longmire, senior vice president at Brouillard Communications, a division of J. Walter Thompson, has said: "The last decade has seen about one of every six Fortune 500 corporations disappear as an independent entity. This can be both distracting and motivational for a CEO. And it's CEOs we deal with in image advertising."

So the CEO of a takeover target will run corporate image advertising to keep the stock price up. A study conducted by Brouillard shows that financial analysts and portfolio managers admit to being influenced by a company's reputation, and "advertising is one way a company builds reputation."

Image advertising is also important in communicating continuity in merged or acquired businesses and especially during and after a takeover. In these stressful situations, customers, suppliers, and employees alike tend to be apprehensive. They want to be told what has happened, what is happening, and what's going to happen. They want to be reassured.

Whatever the situation—and sometimes changing times alone are enough to demand a change in name—image advertising can play a major role in taking a corporation safely over the potentially rough road of implementing a new corporate identity.

Image vs. Identity

But before we start examining some pertinent case studies, it's important to clear up a common misunderstanding—a confusion in terminology. When it comes to the perception of a business or industry, we employ two similar terms that are very often confused and used incorrectly. These are *corporate image* and *corporate identity*.

Exactly what is the difference between them, how are they related, and when do you use each?

MAKE A VISUAL STATEMENT

The basic elements of corporate identity are the name and logo (sometimes called *mark* or *symbol*) of the company. It is the planned visual elements in their many varied applications that are used to distinguish one corporation from all the others—the use of the company name and logo on stationery and business cards, on building and vehicle signs, point-of-purchase displays, collateral materials, and, of course, in advertising. (A complete checklist of corporate identity materials may be found in Appendix D.)

In other words, corporate identity is a visual statement of who and what a company is. Because this statement indicates how a corporation views itself, it also bears sharply on how the world in general will perceive the company.

Quoting Anne Fisher in a 1986 Fortune magazine article:

> . . . Sara Lee Corp . . . changed from Consolidated Foods. . . . The old name was not only humdrum but also misleading. Since the Kitchens of Sara Lee Division accounts for less than 10 percent of sales, the name Sara Lee seems an odd choice. But management picked it with image in mind. Among consumers surveyed . . . before the name change, 98 percent recognized the name Sara Lee and 94 percent associated it with high quality.[1]

BE SEEN AND REMEMBERED

In *The Marketing Handbook* Elinor Selame writes:

> [The corporate symbol] is the visible, easily recognizable face of a living, complex business machine. It allows the public to see who produces the goods or services they are buying and is therefore the foundation upon which corporate identity is built.
>
> The symbol becomes the focal or rallying point of the corporation. It is the banner under which a president gathers his or her employees to meet the public.
>
> One of the first identity goals of any commercial enterprise is to be seen and then remembered. In today's fast-paced, heavily populated society, to be seen and remembered is half the business battle.[2]

---

[1]"Spiffing Up the Corporate Image," Anne Fisher, *Fortune,* July 1986.

[2]"A New Corporate Identity," Elinor Selame, *The Marketing Handbook,* Edwin E. Bobrow and Mark D. Bobrow, Dow Jones-Irwin, 1985.

A company's visual statement can be an important confidence builder that leads to sales. The familiar red and white can of Campbell's Soup and Nabisco's ubiquitous red triangle are good examples of the visual identity that says "Buy me! You know you can trust me." But that look must go along with an established and positive image. Incidentally, it's interesting to note that Nabisco's red triangle has survived numerous mergers and acquisitions. A succession of managements recognized a valuable marketing tool when they saw it. And they have kept using it.

IMPACT OF THE PLANNED AND THE UNPLANNED

Corporate image, as opposed to corporate identity, is the combined impact on an observer of all the planned—and unplanned—visual and verbal components generated by the corporation or outside influences. You can say that it's the sum total of a company's advertising, and it's also a sudden decline in the price of the company's stock; it's the success of a brand new product line, and it's also the nervous pitch of an inexperienced salesperson; it's the appointment of a new CEO, and it's the company truck driver who stops to help a stranded motorist.

It's anything and everything that influences how a corporation is received and perceived by any and all of its various target publics or by even a single customer. Not the least of these influences may be the corporate advertising image program.

Linking Two Great Companies

In 1985 Ingersoll-Rand announced the acquisition of Textron's Fafnir Bearing Division and its merger with their own Torrington Company. This move created the largest broad line bearing manufacturer in the United States, fifth largest worldwide.

There couldn't have been better reasons for a corporate campaign. Two sets of similar customers, distributors, and vendors needed to be told of the merger with all of its implications and ramifications. Ingersoll-Rand shareholders needed to be informed of the merger's many advantages. And employees of both companies needed to be assured that although departmental duplications would create some natural job shakeout, fallout would be kept to a minimum.

Each company had been a leader in its own field—Torrington in the development and manufacture of needle bearings, and Fafnir in precision ball bearings. Now their merger would create a synergism, making the combined companies even stronger and more dominant in the marketplace than the two had been separately. In fact it was estimated at the time that "one plus one" would equal "five" when it came to assessing the global market strength forged by joining Torrington and Fafnir. And this new strength and capability were the basic message that had to be communicated to their various target audiences.

BIRTH OF A MARK

Initial announcement of the merger, in the fall of 1985, was an eight-page color supplement. It told the story of the two companies—their histories, products, markets, along with in-depth interviews with their presidents—and was mass mailed to the combined Torrington and Fafnir lists.

This was followed in early 1986 by the first ad in a new corporate image campaign. The two-page spread (see illustration) was headed: "The biggest merger in bearing history has occurred." The striking color photograph showed a typical Torrington needle bearing linked with a typical Fafnir ball bearing. This particular art approach was only one of several concepts proposed, but focus groups of designers and purchasing agents kept coming back to it. "Everybody liked it," says Ted Rosinski, Torrington's manager of marketing communications. "I think it was the mystique of 'how did you link the two bearings?' Our primary audience is the engineer, the designer, so something like this attracted them."

The second ad in the series was also symbolic, featuring the basic roller, representative of the Torrington business, and the ball, representing the Fafnir business, held together, touching. The headline read: "Two great centers of bearing technology have come together." The two linked bearings, artwork for the first ad, were now smaller, repositioned above the ad's signature as a corporate mark. (See illustration.) It is still Torrington's symbol, offering tremendous recognition value. The signature itself in those first ads showed both the Torrington and the Fafnir names as further evidence of the joining together of the two companies. The corporate name, however, was and is The Torrington Company.

"However," says Rosinski, "we feel very strongly about keeping both names active. Each has such a long tradition and following. As a result, the Fafnir name continues importantly as one of three company brands."

Ads ran in *Business Week* and other leading business publications as well as in key design and purchasing magazines. This campaign ran for almost two years until Torrington felt that the market had been covered sufficiently, and that all of their publics were now fully aware of the merger. From the beginning the ads had offered a free 16-page color brochure and also carried reader service numbers. Inquiry levels were high, resulting in a broad distribution of the booklet.

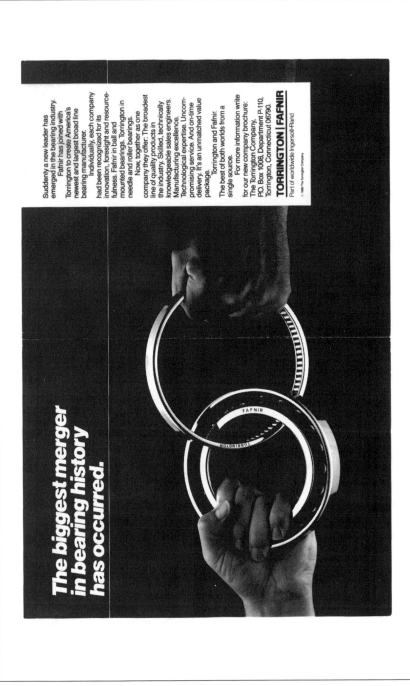

Courtesy of The Torrington Company.

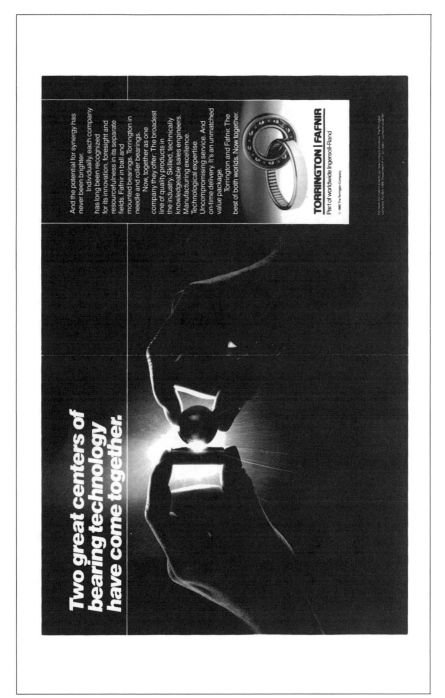

Courtesy of The Torrington Company.

Courtesy of The Torrington Company.

Courtesy of The Torrington Company.

Courtesy of The Torrington Company.

Courtesy of The Torrington Company.

ANOTHER GENERATION OF IMAGE ADS

In 1987 Torrington began a new series of two-page color ads (see illustrations), combining corporate image with the basic business of promoting product, and running in primary business-to-business publications. These ads featured the phrase "The next generation" in headlines and also as a tag line beneath the logo. The thrust of these ads was to show how the new Torrington could better serve the future of both specific markets and industry in general. Advertisements were illustrated dramatically, and carried such headlines as: "Your next generation of paper mill bearings will live a lot longer"; "The next generation of automobiles will be more responsive"; and "The next generation of replacement bearings will make you more productive."

KEEP STIRRING THE POT

Torrington's philosophy, according to Rosinski, is that "it's not just image advertising alone that counts. It's keeping the company image alive and well by constantly doing *something*. It may be a news release, a catalog, a new selling piece, a distributor promotion, a video—whatever. But keep stirring the pot. Let them know you're there, and they'll remember your name."

In 1990, Torrington introduced a new image campaign. These ads dropped the "Next Generation" theme. They were developed from ads on serving the future of different industries to more specific case histories on how Torrington has solved specific problems for specific companies.

These four-color spreads, appearing in leading business and trade publications, feature high-quality, dramatic photography and headlines such as: "This operation cut out 22 painful weeks for Cincinnati Milacron"; and "When a major paper producer lost six $50,000 bearings, this is what we found." Copy is interesting and informative, but sells Torrington as well as specific product applications. (See illustrations.)

Rosinski concludes, "It's not just customers and distributors who respond to such a program. It can also attract better employees and help hold them by building their pride in their company and their work. After all, isn't that where corporate image should really start—with the worker who takes pride in what he does?"

No One Knew CSX from XYZ

The Torrington-Fafnir merger was easy and clean, at least from a communication standpoint. After all, both companies were in the same basic business, looking to reach similar markets. And both names were known and respected. The surviving Torrington Company needed no explanation, and while Fafnir was eliminated from the corporate name, it was kept active for marketing purposes.

The merger of Chessie System Railroads and Seaboard Coast Line Industries and the resultant renaming of the combined corporation was a different kettle of fish. Says Edwin S. Edel: "On October 31, 1980, CSX Corporation didn't even exist. Twenty-four hours later it was the largest transportation and natural resource company in the nation. But the nation didn't know it. And CSX was hardly a household word."[3]

In fact, no one knew CSX from XYZ. They were just another three-letter corporation, with a confusing name and without any particular reputation.

How CSX built image with target audiences is a subject for a later chapter, but at this point it's apropos to examine at least their method of name selection. According to Edel:

> During the two years of Interstate Commerce Commission reviews and hearings leading up to approval of the merger, the working letters *CSX* had been assigned to the project: the *C* for Chessie, the *S* for Seaboard, and the *X* as the multiplication symbol, since the two merged companies would have even greater capabilities combined than they would individually.
>
> In time, the name gained wide acceptance internally, and by the time the question was asked "What should we call this new corporation?" the consensus was "What's wrong with calling it CSX?"

And CSX it was. However, management understood that CSX's recognition factor was at ground zero, and this problem was further compounded by the fact that a number of other soundalike, three-letter companies were already in existence. Thus it isn't surprising that CSX continued with the Chessie and Seaboard names in marketing efforts, including them even in signing their new advertising. How this image campaign was constructed and what results it had—especially with the financial and business communities—are discussed in Chapter 5.

GTE: Another Confused Identity

One more firm that's worked hard to get the public to know and understand better the company behind the initials is GTE. Formed in 1935 as General Telephone

---

[3] "The Joy of CSX—Forming a Corporate Identity," Edwin Edel, *Crosscurrents,* Vol. 12, 1983.

Corporation, the company was the result of a reorganization of a utility holding corporation, and was comprised of more than a dozen local telephone companies, each operating under a different name.

With the acquisition in 1959 of Sylvania Electric Products, the company became General Telephone and Electronics Corporation, and in the mid-1960s joined the alphabet parade as GT&E. But in the following years a variety of names and logos and a continuing strong identity with Sylvania tended only to blur the company's public image. There was no clear brand name, no clear corporate identity.

In the 1970s, the company's agency, Doyle, Dane & Bernbach, came up with the mnemonic line: "Gee! No, GTE." Its simplicity was a natural and its success almost instant. Used to promote the company's dramatic technological and telecommunications achievements, the line soon began separating GTE from its old stodgy and confused image.

RECOGNITION LEVEL RAISED

Research indicated that the new advertising theme helped raise the recognition level of the corporation's initials almost at once. Seven years later, tracking studies showed that campaign awareness had been increased 250 percent. One hundred percent of respondents knew that GTE was in the communications business, with lesser numbers recognizing that the company was in lighting and precision materials as well.

Good things have a way of coming to an end, however. Listen to Rupert Smith, GTE's advertising director.

> Research began telling us two things. First, that our name awareness had pretty much peaked out. We had been roughly at 90 percent awareness by the general public and at nearly 100 percent by the business community. But it started to turn down and dropped into the mid-80s shortly after.
>
> Secondly, we conducted personality research. We discovered there were three primary perceptions of GTE as far as personality characteristics were concerned. The first was "traditional," the second, "capable," and the third, "unadventurous." That image just simply wouldn't cut it in today's competitive environment.
>
> So we set out to create a new corporate advertising campaign. But instead of following our usual 'from top down' procedure, i.e., go to the agency for a creative idea, sell the chairman, and implement, we decided to form an ad hoc committee for this project. This was due in part to a general company move toward more participative management, and partly because if you want support for your program you need involvement.

The GTE committee consisted of representatives from both headquarters and field operations—from the disciplines of marketing, public affairs, and advertising. They fed into the agency GTE's various objectives and goals, and the agency came up with four different campaigns.

All four were presented to the committee, and the committee chose "The Power Is On." The campaign was then pretested and scored very well. It was then submitted to and approved by the president, the chairman, and eventually the board of directors. In the Fall of 1988, GTE launched "The Power Is On."

THREE BROAD GOALS

The new campaign had three broad corporate goals. The first was to *signal change,* to establish that GTE was not the same corporation it was in the past. The second was to *build identity* for GTE, to better communicate who the company was and what businesses it was in. The third was to create a *common thread* throughout all of GTE's various advertising programs.

That common thread, of course, was the signature line: "The Power Is On." Even though each of GTE's six business units has product and service advertising of its own, and employs a variety of creative approaches, they all use that same signature line.

Adds Smith: "A good part of our creative address was to change the previous, outdated personality perceptions of GTE as 'traditional,' 'capable,' and 'unadventurous' to the more positive and contemporary: 'energetic,' 'responsive,' and 'on-the-move'."

EMPLOYEE PREVIEW

Smith continues:

> We made sure that every employee of GTE had an opportunity to see the new campaign and understand the rationale for it before it was ever launched. That's roughly 160,000 employees.
>
> We have a video network throughout the corporation, and we distributed large quantities of video tapes. Every employee had the opportunity to watch. We also had articles in various internal publications, and sent out bulletins. A new section to our corporate identity standards manual was added on the new signature line, giving everyone proper guidelines on its usage.

GTE gets good marks for its employee communications program. Even mergers are discussed with employees. As of this writing, developments on a proposed

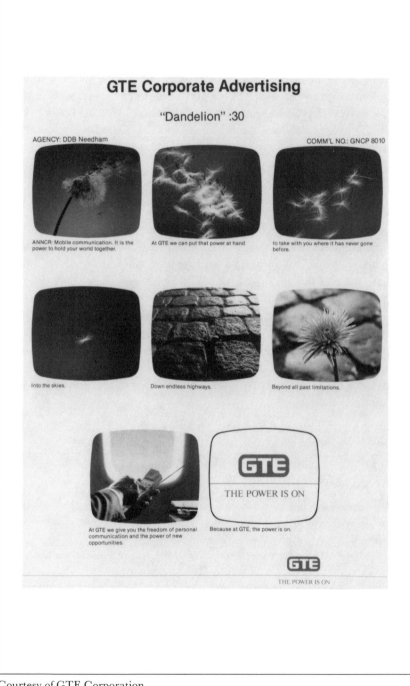

Courtesy of GTE Corporation.

Courtesy of GTE Corporation.

merger with Contel are communicated to employees frequently by GTE's employee communications group. Regular bulletins on the possible merger go out with a dual logo on them—a Contel-GTE logo. That's in addition to the corporate magazine and a variety of other internal communications vehicles.

Keep Looking At the Research

Concludes Smith:

> How long will this campaign last? I don't know. I'll keep looking at the research results. Is it doing what we want it to do? Thus far we're satisfied. We did turn around some declining numbers which was—and usually is—difficult to do. We put the brakes on the downturn and ended up actually turning the numbers up and improving a little bit. We feel real good about it.

Many Reasons for Changing Identity

A merger is often reason enough to change a corporation's name and identity. But there are many other possible motivations. These might include: some shift in long-term corporate strategy; a need to break from the past; to establish the company in particular markets; to reflect major changes in product lines; or to take on a new look after an acquisition or divestiture.

In the case of International Harvester changing its identity to Navistar, there were several good reasons.

First of all, there was a legal obligation to change. When the company's agricultural equipment operations were sold to Tenneco, so also were the rights to the name International Harvester (IH) and its familiar logo. Secondly, since the company was no longer in that business, it needed a new identity in keeping with its new business direction.

There was also confusion in the marketplace, with both companies using the International Harvester name. A name change was the only way to clear up the confusion. Last, but certainly not least, financial troubles at the time made the need for a total change of identity quite real and very much in order.

Teamwork

Teamwork has always been an essential ingredient for business success. International Harvester had a healthy respect for this concept and knew to apply it to the business of their name change.

According to John McDonald, the company's director of communications:

During the first half of the 1980s, IH experienced a wrenching transformation. Just how wrenching can be clearly illustrated with one example. In 1979, IH was a company with approximately $8 billion in sales and roughly 100,000 employees. By 1986, sales were nearly $3.5 billion with only 15,000 employees.

In a crucible fired by severe recession, rocketing interest rates, massive debt, and virtual depression in our major markets, International Harvester fought for its very survival. The experts said it was only a matter of time, and almost everyone else agreed.

But not everyone. That crucible glowed white hot with the pride and determination of employees at a company with a longstanding tradition of success in business. Teamwork, the teamwork of employees, customers, suppliers, lenders, shareholders, retirees and others, would not allow the experts' predictions to come true.

This same sense of teamwork was instrumental in the development of IH's new corporate identity. Hundreds of people were involved, outsiders as well as employees. Central elements of the team were identity consultants Anspach Grossman Portugal, advertising agency Young & Rubicam, public relations counsel Hill and Knowlton, and, of course, IH's own communications department.

Individuals from marketing, sales, engineering, design, human resources, manufacturing, purchasing, investor relations, finance, and every other facet of the organization played significant roles. So too did numerous outside printing, design, and audio-visual firms.

Build a Strong Foundation

Work on the project began in earnest in April 1985. It was soon apparent that the challenge faced was not simply to change a name but to develop an entirely new identity for a 150-year-old company with worldwide recognition.

John McDonald notes: "To help us determine the scope and direction of our project, the first phase of our reidentification program involved opinion research. For approximately two and a half months we conducted interviews with employees, key suppliers, customers, dealers, retirees, lenders, the media, and even our competitors.

"Through this research we gained an understanding of how International Harvester was perceived, what specific identity needs the company had, and what our strengths and weaknesses were. The use of research gave us a strong foundation upon which to build."

WHAT SHOULD A NEW NAME ACCOMPLISH?

Then IH began developing lists of attributes the new name should convey. The name had to capture the spirit of the corporation's true personality and character, and had to articulate the new business focus. What's more, says McDonald, "It needed to describe the company as independent, enduring, confident, lean, disciplined, focused, progressive."

Other criteria required consideration as well. The new name must be legally protectable. It needed to be translated easily into the language of any foreign market where the company might ever do business. And the new name also had to be easy to pronounce, reducing the risk of a negative corporate nickname.

Following these guidelines, a list of more than 3,000 possible names was compiled, of both human and computer generation. It took three months to narrow the list down to a manageable 10 candidates. In mid-October 1985, the name Navistar was selected.

Because research had indicated a widespread acceptance of and equity in their "International" brand of products, the company also decided to retain the brand name. But with the loss of the widely used IH logo, it was necessary to develop a new corporate brand mark and color.

Don't Overlook the Visual Dimension

McDonald describes the graphic design process they followed:

> Having chosen a suitable name, our next challenge was to give it life in graphic form. While words do much to shape a company's personality and image, the "look" of a name—the way it appears on everything from business cards to trucks—plays a major role in directing the meaning the words take on.
>
> We looked at many possible renderings, tried various styles of type and a number of special treatments, to arrive at the best communicative form of Navistar. Initially we tried to use the letter N to highlight the entire word. But in the design finally adopted we dropped the idea of using the N and used the two A's as the key feature of the word.
>
> Since the letter A appears at both the beginning and end of Navistar, the stylized version of the letter adds graphic symmetry to the word. You'll also note that the bold typeface and slanted letters give the word strength and a sense of motion—Navistar isn't standing still!

Color was another element considered, and a deep blue was chosen for a number of reasons:

1. Psychologically, blue tends to indicate stability and generally has a positive effect on people.

2. Blue also signifies strength.

3. It has good recognition value.

4. It was felt that blue was a diplomatic color many people would find pleasing.

Developed, too, was a new symbol for International. After much research and study, a mark called the "Diamond Road" was created. Designed to be a powerful graphic, the "Diamond Road" features a double diamond configuration with "The Road to the Future" through the middle. The companion color chosen was orange. This is a hot color psychologically, and it implies a healthy aggressiveness in the marketplace. Navistar was ready to "surge ahead on the road to the future." (See illustration.)

Start with Internal Communication
On January 7, 1986, the announcement was made. Employees were the first audience chosen to receive information regarding the company's new identity. They were addressed by both the chairman and the president, live, by satellite. Afterwards they were given complete information kits and special mementos of the occasion.

Following the morning announcement to employees, a major press conference was held at world headquarters in Chicago. Publicity efforts were based on an approach aimed at, according to John McDonald, "making sure we were caught in the act of doing good." In addition, promotional kits were sent to arrive at each dealer location on the morning of announcement day.

Fast External Follow-Up
Advertising for this new corporate identity began the day after the announcement and centered around a very intensive, high-profile image campaign. The campaign was highly visual and utilized network television as well as print and radio. A TV commercial appeared over a five-week span on such programs as the NFL Playoffs, "60 Minutes," "20/20," "Nightline," and evening news shows. The sound track from the commercial served as radio copy.

The opening gun in the print campaign was a three-page blockbuster with the headline: "On the very first day of its existence, this will be a 3.5 billion dollar company with the number one position in its industry."

Copy was filled with hard facts about where the company had been and where it was going. Color photography of a sunrise and an International truck symbolized a bright new day for Navistar. The tag line "Navistar . . . the rebirth of International Harvester" told the story. (See illustration.)

Courtesy of Navistar International Transportation Corp.

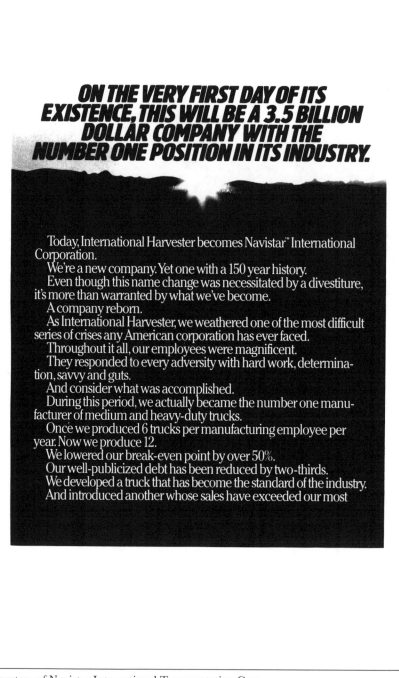

ON THE VERY FIRST DAY OF ITS EXISTENCE, THIS WILL BE A 3.5 BILLION DOLLAR COMPANY WITH THE NUMBER ONE POSITION IN ITS INDUSTRY.

Today, International Harvester becomes Navistar™ International Corporation.

We're a new company. Yet one with a 150 year history.

Even though this name change was necessitated by a divestiture, it's more than warranted by what we've become.

A company reborn.

As International Harvester, we weathered one of the most difficult series of crises any American corporation has ever faced.

Throughout it all, our employees were magnificent.

They responded to every adversity with hard work, determination, savvy and guts.

And consider what was accomplished.

During this period, we actually became the number one manufacturer of medium and heavy-duty trucks.

Once we produced 6 trucks per manufacturing employee per year. Now we produce 12.

We lowered our break-even point by over 50%.

Our well-publicized debt has been reduced by two-thirds.

We developed a truck that has become the standard of the industry.

And introduced another whose sales have exceeded our most

Courtesy of Navistar International Transportation Corp.

optimistic projections by at least 50%.

All while the experts were predicting our imminent doom.

Of course, there are challenges that still face us.

But we begin our new enterprise in an enviable position.

We're expecting sales this year of 3.5 billion dollars.

On our first day of business, we're in the top quarter of the *Fortune 500.* We're already the industry leader.

Our International™ trucks are known throughout the world for unmatched quality and low cost of ownership.

We're developing innovative new products and services to help our customers compete profitably in deregulated markets.

We're lean, aggressive, forward-looking and independent. Not to mention tested.

We're Navistar International.

A brand new company of nearly 15,000 people who are very proud of all you've just read.

NAVISTAR

The rebirth of International Harvester.

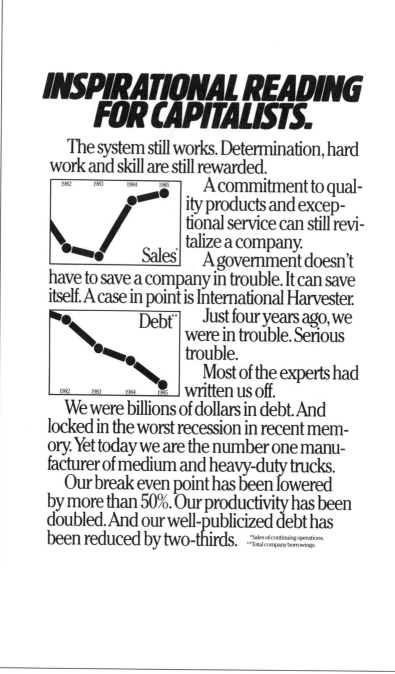

INSPIRATIONAL READING FOR CAPITALISTS.

The system still works. Determination, hard work and skill are still rewarded.

A commitment to quality products and exceptional service can still revitalize a company.

Sales*

A government doesn't have to save a company in trouble. It can save itself. A case in point is International Harvester.

Debt**

Just four years ago, we were in trouble. Serious trouble.

Most of the experts had written us off.

We were billions of dollars in debt. And locked in the worst recession in recent memory. Yet today we are the number one manufacturer of medium and heavy-duty trucks.

Our break even point has been lowered by more than 50%. Our productivity has been doubled. And our well-publicized debt has been reduced by two-thirds.

*Sales of continuing operations.
**Total company borrowings.

Courtesy of Navistar International Transportation Corp.

The difference was people. Our people.

People in offices, in factories and in the field.

People who didn't need to be motivated because they motivated themselves.

People who responded to crises with courage, discipline and savvy.

And also the people who we knew were pulling for us.

Our customers, our dealers, our suppliers, the financial community and even our competitors.

We proved that nothing is impossible to a corporation that believes in itself. And that a 150 year old institution can be lean, forward-looking and independent.

Recently we changed our name from International Harvester to Navistar International Corporation.

The change was necessitated by a divestiture.

But we believe it was warranted by the company we've become.

Adam Smith would have loved it.

NAVISTAR™
The rebirth of International Harvester.

Subsequent ads offered headlines like: "Miracles still happen." "Inspirational reading for capitalists"; and "What do you call 15,000 people who survived billions of dollars of debt, the worst recession in recent memory, were written off by most of the experts, and still came out on top? Your neighbors."

Copy talked about Navistar's employees and the value of team effort and enterprise. The "Neighbors" ad ran in newspapers serving cities where they had plants or facilities, and was designed to raise the identity and comfort level of employees while thanking them for a job well done.

Principal media for the campaign were the *Wall Street Journal, USA Today,* the *New York Times, Fortune, Forbes, Business Week,* and *Time.*

Even when the initial announcement program was complete, Navistar continued its image advertising. New black-and-white ads (see illustration), using a variety of illustrative techniques, featured long but highly readable copy, and such headlines as: "We're a little bit different than most new companies"; "We had a strong motivation to embrace change"; and "How a 9 month old company can make a product with a 15 year reputation for quality."

Did It Work?

Did all the effort pay off? Says John McDonald: "In a word—yes! Using two more words—and how! The reception Navistar received, from all constituencies, was almost unbelievable. As expected we heard from some people who didn't like the name or our new look. The overwhelming majority, however, were captivated by Navistar and what it represents."

How did Navistar know this? In a lot of ways. Immediately following the announcement, for example, major stories on the change appeared in publications like the *Wall Street Journal,* the *New York Times, USA Today,* the *Chicago Tribune, Fortune, Business Week, Time,* and *Newsweek,* along with many others. Virtually all of them were positive. And so were the stories that appeared in the trade press.

At the same time, network and local television stations were also running segments on the change, and once again the editorial feel was decidedly positive.

Soon after the advertising began, letters began pouring in to Navistar. The general message seemed to be along these lines: "Congratulations on your ad today in (publication name) and more importantly on the story it tells!"

And what were employees saying? A typical comment was: "I think the new name really hit me for the first time when I saw the commercial. I thought, 'that's my company and I'm part of it.' I felt really good."

Navistar, of course, also conducted thorough opinion research. The story was still the same. Research indicated that the company had reached over 84 percent of its target audience, and they could recall the content of the ads.

WHAT DO YOU CALL 15,000 PEOPLE WHO SURVIVED BILLIONS OF DOLLARS OF DEBT, THE WORST RECESSION IN RECENT MEMORY, WERE WRITTEN OFF BY MOST OF THE EXPERTS, AND STILL CAME OUT ON TOP?

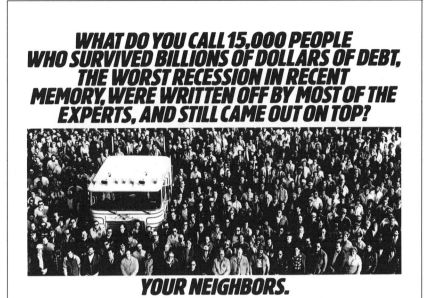

YOUR NEIGHBORS.

They work here in town. For the company that until today was known as International Harvester.

Together they weathered one of the most difficult series of crises any American corporation has ever faced.

Through it all, they were magnificent.

They responded to every adversity with hard work, determination, savvy and guts.

And consider what they accomplished.

Despite the hardships, they helped us become the industry leader, with trucks and engines known throughout the world for quality and efficiency.

Our manufacturing productivity has been doubled.

And our well-publicized debt has been cut by two-thirds.

Recently a divestiture has forced us to change our name.

So today IH is becoming Navistar™ International Corporation.

A brand new company of nearly 15,000 people.

To you, they're neighbors. To us, they're heroes.

NAVISTAR™
The rebirth of International Harvester.

Courtesy of Navistar International Transportation Corp.

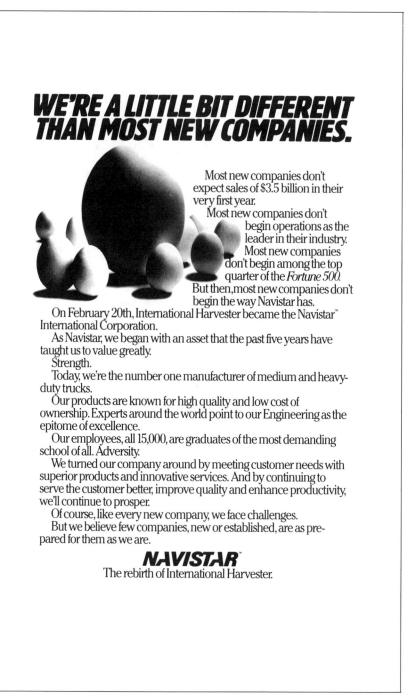

Among financial analysts—a primary target—Navistar reached over 88 percent. And among this group, the "favorable opinion" rating improved by more than 20 percentage points.

Of 250 International dealers surveyed, 93 percent said their customers had mentioned seeing or hearing the advertisements. Shareholders approved the name by 98 percent! Even company recruiters on college campuses felt the campaign's impact. They now had waiting lists of applicants for cancellations on their interviewing schedule.

A final word from McDonald: "Perhaps some of the most sincere endorsements came from other companies, asking about our identity change while making preparations for a change of their own. All in all, it was a tough, demanding, time-consuming project—but an extremely satisfying one as well."

Bristol-Myers Squibb: The Standard of Quality

Acquisition, merger, or reorganization does not always mean the demise of some well-known and respected corporate name. Nor do all identity changes require long, complex procedures. When the stockholders of Squibb Corporation and Bristol-Myers Company voted in October 1989 to merge into a single corporation, the choice of a new name seemed obvious. The next day Bristol-Myers Squibb Company became officially the new but easily recognized and remembered name for the merged companies.

The combination created one of the strongest companies in the world, with leadership positions in four core business areas—pharmaceuticals, consumer products, nutritionals, and medical devices. "Individually," Mr. Richard Gelb, Chairman and CEO, notes, "Bristol-Myers Company and Squibb Corporation already have accomplished a great deal and set new standards for excellence both in product research and development and in business conduct and achievement. But together, we will become more than simply the sum of our individual parts."

A single black-and-white corporate ad told the whole story. Headlined "*Take Two . . .*" the ad featured two tablets, each bearing the name of one of the two merging companies (see illustration). Four short paragraphs of copy made the key points.

This ad, appearing in the *New York Times* and other newspapers in areas where the two merging companies have major installations, spearheaded a total communications program. Press releases, several executive staff bulletins to employees, draft letters to various constituencies, the annual report and a quarterly report, and articles in several issues of their internal employee publication, *Bristol-Myers Squibb World,* all helped tell the merger story.

Courtesy of Bristol-Myers Squibb Company.

Nor was this company any stranger to image advertising. As far back as 1921 Squibb had run the classic: "The Priceless Ingredient" (see illustration). A collaborative effort of Theodore Weicker, Sr., later chairman of E.R. Squibb & Sons, and Raymond Rubicam, founder of Young & Rubicam, variations of "The Priceless Ingredient" appeared in Squibb advertisements until the 1940s. It is a classic and has been reprinted many times in advertising collections and textbooks.

When Identity Does Not Change after Acquisition

A holding company needs corporate image, too—a single consistent image to be reflected by all its member companies. This is often, however, a rather loose arrangement, with each participating company creating its own image within the framework of some predetermined corporate mission.

Take First Michigan Bank Corporation, for example. They have a corporate mission statement, intended to set the tone for each member bank's own advertising. The statement reads: "To serve profitably as a leading and progressive financial corporation of high quality, offering services in a superior manner that are responsive to the needs of our customers . . . for the benefit of our stockholders, communities, and employees."

Despite this common mission, each of First Michigan Bank's independent community banks retains its own identity and controls its own marketing budget. They select their own media and decide on their own product and pricing.

There is a centralized marketing department, however, to ensure similar looks for all their ads. Although each bank signs its advertising with its own name, they all also feature the same common FMB logo.

Comments Thomas Moore, FMB vice president for corporate planning:

A limited First Michigan Bank umbrella campaign has helped set the stage for our individual banks by introducing the FMB logo to their customers, thus strengthening each bank's overall image of quality and solidity.

We have wrestled with the issues of centralized and decentralized marketing and image creation for a number of years. Image is important to us and will, I'm sure, continue to be.

Meanwhile, it seems a key factor in tying a group of independent community banks together as one solid and successful financial institution.

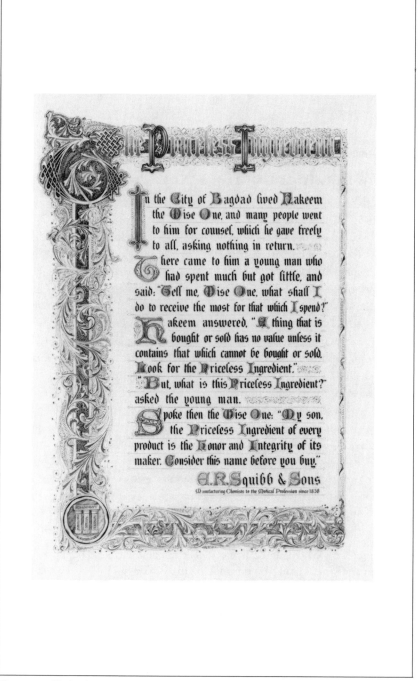

Courtesy of Bristol-Myers Squibb Company.

THE ROUND-THE-CLOCK SALESPERSON

In banking, as in many businesses, the product is often identical to competition's. The only way to stand apart may be in terms of corporate image. Sometimes that's a tough sale.

But it's a sale that's almost always worth making. A winning image offers much to any corporation's success, whether they sell a parity product or some highly unique item. And for this winning image, a strong, positive identity can make a really significant contribution. A memorable corporate name, a striking logo, and compatible corporate graphics can be the most cost-effective marketing expenditures a company can make. It's like having a permanent round-the-clock salesperson. Each time the name, logo, or package is recognized, equity in the corporate identity increases. And as identity builds, it becomes easier to establish an appropriate image for the corporation.

Image may not be "the product" for every corporation, but it can have a very positive effect on both product sales and the overall success of the company.

Research tells us that when a corporation has a good image the public is more likely to assume that it produces good products—and the public is more likely to buy and even pay more for those products.

The following chapter addresses this in detail, and covers some of the ways an image advertising campaign can actively support brand sales.

CHAPTER FOUR

Pre-selling Target Markets:
Image and Brand— The Dynamic Duo

''I don't know who you are.

I don't know your company.

I don't know your company's product.

I don't know what your company stands for.

I don't know your company's customers.

I don't know your company's record.

I don't know your company's reputation.

Now—what was it you wanted to sell me?''

Whatever other purpose an image campaign may have, such advertising almost always helps prepare the marketplace for the sale of the product. McGraw-

Hill's classic "I don't know who you are" ad, prepared originally by Fuller & Smith & Ross, has been telling prospective advertisers about this benefit for years. (See illustration.)

When corporate advertising is tied directly into product advertising, especially in highly competitive markets, the result is often an improved sales picture. Corporate advertising, of course, isn't product advertising, but it can create the right environment of familiarity and confidence to help product advertising performance. A company's image, or whatever reputation people associate with a brand, is indeed highly critical to sales, because it's tied in directly to how comfortable customers feel about buying and using a product.

Products change from year to year, and consumers want to be sure that the company stands behind them, that it still makes quality products, and that it will be there should problems arise. Some sort of marriage between image and product ad campaigns is essential if a company wants to reap full value from each as they work toward separate but compatible objectives.

According to Ron Rhody, senior vice president at the Bank of America: "All good corporate advertising should have a product. You're wasting your money otherwise. Corporate advertising should advertise the sale of your product—only you're selling the store, not the product itself."[1]

Sell the Sizzle

Phillip A. Bossert, director of special promotions at *Business Week,* has said: *"Business Week* helped to pioneer business advertising, and since we started in 1929 we've carried a lot of corporate advertising. But trends in corporate advertising have changed with the times.

"There was a period when many companies were doing social responsibility advertising like 'protecting fish in the Salmon River.' Now we see image ads designed to help move goods."

That's what we've found in the case studies examined so far. Although the stated objective of a campaign may have been to build new awareness of a company or to announce a name change or accomplish some other corporate mission, the end result in just about every instance has been to help sell a product or service.

It's not by accident that Wausau and The Travelers have sold a lot of insurance through well-conceived corporate image advertising. Chemical Bank, J.P.

---

[1]"Corporate Advertising," Michael Winkleman, *Public Relations Journal,* December 1985.

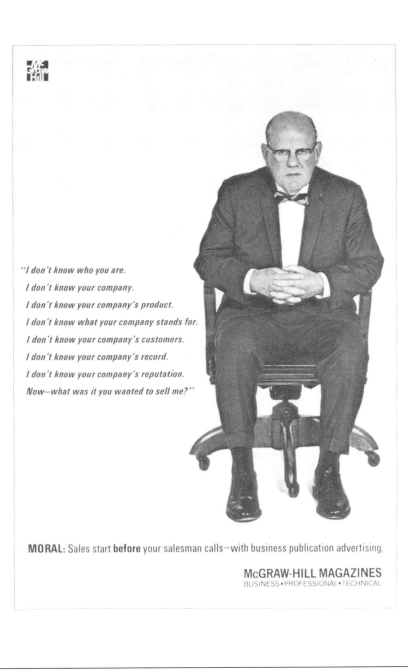

Morgan, Du Pont, Torrington, and many, many others, too, have discovered that selling the sizzle really does help sell the steak.

A recent study by *Time,* conducted by Yankelovich, Skelly and White, also concludes that product advertising is more valuable when coupled with corporate advertising: "Regardless of how high one's products are held in esteem among a responsive public, this image is not transferable automatically to management confidency or to positive attitudes about the corporation's future direction. Conversely, a corporate campaign teamed up with product advertising can result in higher advertising recall and all other corporate traits measured."

There are, of course, many corporations whose products *are* their image. This is particularly true in the field of packaged goods. Ivory Soap, Duncan Hines, Crest, and Luvs all carry their own respective images, basically unaffected by any corporate Procter & Gamble (P&G) image. Those product images, however, all make contributions to the overall P&G corporate image.

General Foods does not need to run image advertising to support their Birds Eye or Maxwell House brands, nor does General Mills for its Betty Crocker line. These products do quite well for themselves, and also lend an aura of quality and success to their parent companies.

There are times when even leading brands can use corporate image support. The Tylenol tragedy prompted an immediate and well-considered response on the part of Johnson & Johnson. Swift steps were taken to stabilize the situation and begin putting Tylenol sales back on track. Every capsule product made by J & J was quickly removed from store shelves, and all advertising was stopped. Within weeks, Tylenol was re-introduced in new, tamper-proof packaging, and coupons worth $2.50 were distributed to the American public to offset the cost of their replacing old Tylenol packages. Tylenol had rebuilt its image and regained sales momentum in a little more than three months, and J & J's respected image played an important role in the turnaround.

One leading brand, Wrigley's, generally feels that it needs no specific corporate advertising. The brand sells itself. But even Wrigley's, on one occasion, found good use for image. In 1988 Wm. Wrigley Jr. Company employed a corporate television commercial, titled "Share a Little Piece of America," to support the Olympics and emphasize Wrigley's wholesome, all-American image. It undoubtedly made a lot of sales too. (See illustrations.)

A MAGICAL MUSICAL SIGNATURE

On the other hand, there's Nabisco. It has always been an advocate of strong positive corporate identity. We are all familiar with its red triangle logo, featured in every commercial, in every ad, on every package. But when Nabisco

Courtesy of Wm. Wrigley Jr. Company.

Courtesy of Wm. Wrigley Jr. Company.

merged with Standard Brands in 1982, it decided to escalate its corporate image program.

The merger gave Nabisco several new and successful brands that were very familiar to consumers—such as Royal and Fleischmann's—but were not identifiable with Nabisco. Searching for an effective way to identify all of its brands, Nabisco decided upon a musical signature, a magical three-note combination that says *Na-bis-co*. Used in Nabisco's television and radio advertising, these three musical notes echo positively in the shareholder's mind as well as in the consumer's, in the supplier's as well as the employee's.

Nabisco's thrust has always been to identify clearly their corporate name while promoting strong brand franchise names like Oreo and Ritz. But rather than invest in separate corporate advertising, they have integrated their message into brand commercials they would have produced anyway.

IBM: Two Campaigns in One

IBM is another advertiser that uses one campaign to accomplish two ends. Not surprisingly, this single campaign evolved from two separate ones.

The first was designed to reflect a company that employs good people, has an ethical value system, and does good things for society. The second was a kind of market prep advertising that sought to precondition the market to be ready, willing, and anxious to consider buying the IBM brand. Both campaigns were in print and on TV.

One set of ads originated out of IBM's corporate communications department while the other came from the company's marketing organization. Early in 1990 responsibility for both campaigns was assigned to marketing, but corporate communications still provides input on messages and key topics. Separate sources of funding still exist, so that a corporate message gets paid for from one budget and a marketing-oriented message from another. But it's still one series of ads and another of TV commercials, each in its own format, and the total is referred to as the "image" campaign.

At this time, IBM runs four 60-second spots, one a marketing message and three corporate. "If I showed you the four," says Jim Garrity, Director of Advertising, IBM United States, "you might not be able to tell me which is which. In my mind that's good, because we don't believe TV viewers distinguish between the two different kinds of messages. It's a similar situation for the print advertising, although our print ads tend to stress the marketing messages more."

Courtesy of IBM Corporation.

Courtesy of IBM Corporation.

Two Sets of Objectives

The new image campaign, stemming as it does from two separate roots, has parallel sets of objectives. One is to create in the minds of a majority of working adults, ages 25 to 54, and opinion leaders the positive view that IBM is a good company, with good people working for it—that it's an ethical company, committed to making the world a better place.

Says Garrity:

> We'd like to be perceived from a societal point of view as a company that's concerned about important issues, such as the environment or drugs, and that we're doing more than talk or advertise about it—that we actually put people, money, technical resources into a solution.
>
> From the standpoint of marketing, we'd like to turn around some notions about us as a company, to have more people willing to consider buying IBM. Unfortunately, many important audiences have stereotypical views.
>
> They think IBM is interested only in large businesses, not small. They think we're interested in selling to data processing departments, not professionals and users. They think we've got good large systems, but not the broad range of smaller systems tailored to their needs.

Like most corporations of any size, IBM relies a great deal on research to guide advertising plans. Research established the platform for this new campaign, and it has set the benchmark of attitudes and awareness against which they track their campaign goals. A relatively new IBM department, Communications Research, has been able to show that pre-testing is highly projectible, eliminating many surprises.

"Research tells us," concludes Garrity, "that some perceive us as not listening well, not responding to needs. Actually, our thrust is to become more market driven, to understand our customers' needs, and then deliver those needs."

The campaign wear-out factor for most advertisers usually happens internally much sooner than it does externally. People pay more attention to their own company's advertising, and after a while may say: "Are we still running that?" But in the case of IBM, the print ads, with their striking Richard Avedon black-and-white photos, as well as the TV 60s, seem to have a long run ahead.

Starch scores indicate that the print advertising is not wearing out. People don't look at an ad and say "I've seen that before." Pre- and post-testing tell IBM that their television commercials have "long legs" too, and should be effective in building acceptance and supporting sales for years.

When It's a Long Time between Purchases

Sometimes image advertising can have a very specific and direct relationship to product sales. Take the case of Goodyear. In the late 1970s, its chairman went to Brouillard Communications, posing the problem: "How do we maintain and build consumer preference for Goodyear tires during the long intervals between tire purchases?" He was particularly interested in finding out whether corporate advertising might help.

The tire purchase cycle is every three years. During the period when someone actively looks for a new set of tires, they will have a brief perception of retail tire advertising. This awareness might last a little longer as far as brand advertising goes. Goodyear was looking for a layer of corporate advertising that could bolster their product effort, help bridge the awareness gap across the three-year purchase cycle.

Brouillard's solution was an advertising campaign that starred the famous Goodyear blimp. Their research indicated that the blimp was synonomous with Goodyear, so the plan was to feature it in lighthearted dramatizations reflecting the dependable high quality of Goodyear tires.

"WE'VE GOT THE BLIMP BEHIND US"

Both television and print were used, with the print taking its direction from the TV. The theme line used thoughout the campaign was, "We've got the blimp behind us," and the visual reinforced the slogan. A typical commercial featured two nuns driving on a wet, slippery road. They're not worried because they know they "have the blimp behind us," and there, sure enough, is the Goodyear blimp right behind their car. One nun says, "It's good to have friends in high places." Final words from the voice-over are, as in all the commercials, "Come up to Goodyear."

What Goodyear and Brouillard found was a dramatic increase in consumer recall of Goodyear advertising. Based on this new awareness, Goodyear felt that there was indeed an important correlation between the image campaign and product sales.

According to Douglas Longmire, senior vice president of Brouillard, "In fact, we took this campaign and ran it as a test in Canada. Recall was so good that Goodyear replaced their regular tire advertising in Canada with the new campaign, and it did a great job of brand-name registration, which up to then had been a particular problem in Canada."

GOODYEAR AS A PERSON

At about that time, in 1982, Brouillard looked to develop the perceived "personality" of Goodyear by borrowing a research technique from packaged goods advertising. Using the familiar man-on-the-street approach, Brouillard interviewed a number of people regarding their impressions of both Goodyear and their competitor, Michelin. The key question was: "If Goodyear (or Michelin) were a person, what would he be like?" Answers indicated that Goodyear was well liked and considered dependable, sort of an all-American guy, but was also thought of as older and unexciting, with not very many ideas. "Monsieur" Michelin's image on the other hand was exciting, innovative, and much more sophisticated.

NO LONGER A TIRE COMPANY

Major changes were now taking place at Goodyear. For one thing a new chairman, Robert E. Mercer, was appointed. Then, too, the market had changed. Tire growth had slowed down and stabilized at 1–2 percent per year. Mercer was aware of the man-on-the-street research and, looking for ways to attract investors, saw that it was necessary to build a new reputation, one more innovative and growth oriented.

One solution would be to diversify more, but it was important that such a move be communicated to Goodyear's various target audiences. Their world must be told that Goodyear was no longer just a tire company, that it was deeply involved in plastics, chemicals, aerospace, and a wide range of other things the public did not normally associate with Goodyear.

Communicate the Excitement

The task for advertising now was to highlight Goodyear's diversification and many product developments, to communicate the company's spirit of innovation. The agency's answer was to feature product breakthroughs, using unconventional visuals to dramatize a new sense of excitement and growth at Goodyear.

The creative platform called for an animation technique that was equally effective in print and television. Ads featured a stylized cartoon of three faces, referred to as "they" and representing conventional wisdom. The little man in each ad is the Goodyear Man, and he puts "they" in their place by pointing out "all the dynamite things you can do when you don't listen to what 'they' say." Typical copy reads: "They say there's nothing better than steel for making airplane brakes. But Goodyear said, 'We'll see about that,' and went on to build brakes made of carbon. They stop like steel, but weigh a lot less and last three times as long. So planes can save money coming and going.''

Small Space Units Can Deliver Impact

The media buy was a little different for a corporate campaign. Small, square, one-third-page units were chosen to deliver more impact and more frequency without increasing the budget. These ads could run in various combinations and formats, with each unit emphasizing a different product development. Run individually, each would dominate its page, and a series of three or four on succeeding pages could hardly be overlooked. And when two units to a page were run on facing pages, the ads gave the effect of a color spread for substantially less.

This campaign ran for two years, and then, in 1986, the man-on-the-street study was repeated for comparison with the 1982 benchmark. Results were gratifying. Goodyear had kept its characteristics of honesty, reliability, and family orientation, but was now looked upon as being 15 years younger and more active, committed to new ideas and growth, able to change with the times. "He" was open-minded, a good listener, involved with many important technologies, and a good leader with a sense of humor. Goodyear's perceived personality had livened up markedly, and advertising was given a large measure of credit.

Michelin's image was still sophisticated, but now it had expanded to that of a jet-setter with expensive Italian-cut clothes, unmarried, and a little more remote, not nearly as friendly and well-meaning as Goodyear. He worked hard and knew his stuff; and his product was a good one, although he was dedicated to only one product line.

Back to the Tire Business

At this writing the situation has changed once more for Goodyear. It has a new chairman. Diversification is out, and many of Goodyear's businesses have been sold or cut back drastically. In less than a decade, Goodyear has completed the cycle, going from a tire company image to a diversified image and back again to a tire company.

Although the company may have returned to its core business, it still wants to retain its newfound reputation for innovation and growth, open-mindedness, and worldwide capability.

It's impossible to determine at this point what effect some new campaign might have on Goodyear's future success. But don't bet against the power of image advertising . . . or doubt that image can "set the table" for product sales.

Courtesy of The Goodyear Tire and Rubber Company.

Amoco Chemical: Reaching the "New People"

Every year there are thousands of people arriving fresh on the scene—new entrants to the work force, people who have just been promoted, or who have shifted jobs. Most of them are potential new customers for some product or service. They can be very influential but may not know much about your company or what you sell.

Amoco Chemical calls them the "new people," and they are an important target of Amoco's corporate advertising. Says Sanford C. Schulert, director of marketing communications:

> Our corporate advertising program begins a vital communication process with these "new people." It makes them aware we're the kind of helpful company they can turn to. It familiarizes them with our position in the industry.
>
> Corporate advertising accomplishes this task for us far more cost-effectively than can be done with sales calls and management contacts alone.

The results of Amoco's corporate advertising program speak for themselves. In 1988 alone, the company received over 10,000 inquiries for more information. These responses represent a tremendous opportunity, an entree to many potential new customers.

HAND IN HAND WITH PRODUCT ADVERTISING

At Amoco corporate advertising's job is to increase awareness of the company among industrial managers as a leading supplier of a wide range of innovative, high-quality products.

It communicates that Amoco Chemical understands the quality process and that they are responsive and stand behind their products with technical assistance and dependable follow-through. "More and more, in today's world," adds Schulert, "prospects want to know what we stand for—not just what we make. Our corporate advertising fills that role.

"At the same time, it keeps our established customer relationships strong, and works hand-in-hand with our product advertising."

Multi-Page Ads Magnify Impact

Two-page magazine ads give impact to the program. Each ad features some newsworthy product innovation illustrating Amoco's ongoing leadership and concern for quality. Thought-provoking text talks about the role Amoco plays in the success of its customers and provides essential product development information. It's combined with dramatic color photography to create a feeling of excitement. (See illustration.)

In addition to these two-page advertisements, Amoco also runs special eight-page inserts in key industry vertical publications. Targeted at such markets as automotive, home products, and recreation, the inserts use a case history format demonstrating related Amoco Chemical products in use in a specific industry.

The inserts deliver added customer impact and readership. As stand-alone pieces, they provide detailed information for management and customer presentations, sales calls, recruitment meetings, and employee orientation seminars.

Amoco's corporate advertising is aimed at industrial managers. Thus the ads are run in business publications reaching that group, including *Business Week* and *Fortune* industrial editions and a variety of leading verticals and international publications.

But Amoco's corporate effort doesn't rely solely on media advertising. An important adjunct is *Chemical Reactions,* a quality house magazine which focuses on innovations based on petrochemical products. Copies are sent to over 60,000 top and middle managers at target companies.

THE REALITY OF PERCEPTION

Amoco Chemical is a corporation that believes in tracking its image periodically, looking for both justification and direction. A recent study indicates that the perception of Amoco is enhanced when managers read the corporate advertising. They are more inclined to view Amoco as a leader and as more innovative. And they are more willing to do business with them.

Other studies, notably one by Yankelovich, Skelly and White, confirm Amoco's strong belief that a judicious combination of corporate and product advertising is the most efficient way to lay the groundwork for new customer development.

International Paper Company: "Send Me a Man Who Reads!"

This concept of corporate image advertising contributing to product sales is certainly not a new one. As far back as 1960, when total corporate advertising expenditures didn't account for even $50 million, a few companies did understand

Courtesy of Amoco Chemical Company.

the sales value of what was then called "institutional advertising." The International Paper Company (IP), with its phenomenally successful "Send me a man who *reads!*" campaign (see illustrations) in *Fortune* and *Reader's Digest,* was one outstanding example.

To quote Richard J. Wiechmann, then advertising director at International Paper:

> Many people used to comment to me about my company's "institutional" advertising program. I was always somewhat puzzled by the word "institutional." IP was not an institution; it was—and still is—a company dependent (as are all companies) on sales. Our advertising program was not institutional. It was a sales program . . . a program designed to help sell not just one product but all of the multitude of products that International Paper made.

A SALES PROBLEM

In fact, this program really came into being because of a sales problem. Up until May of 1960 IP had never advertised nationally. But market conditions were changing, and many of its heretofore largest and best customers had either built or bought their own papermaking facilities. As you can imagine, when a paper company loses a customer large enough to require its own paper mill, it has to sell a lot of smaller prospects to make up the loss in sales volume.

After thorough and careful consideration, IP's management decided to undertake a national advertising program. That decision was made because management had a conviction that advertising would strengthen their selling stance for the years ahead.

"Note that reason," says Wiechmann. "It's a *sales* reason. We fully subscribed to the fundamental principle that advertising's job is to *sell.*

"How did corporate advertising help us with our selling job? The sale of our product depended on more than the product itself. It depended on the *image* our customers had of us as a dependable, resourceful, imaginative supplier. A customer might have been buying hundreds of thousands of dollars' worth of paper a year from us. Orders at this level obviously involved many people in the customer's organization, including their top management. Corporate advertising's role in our case had to be related to what it could do to support this total selling operation."

IP strengthened its selling as it developed strong, favorable public recognition through advertising. That, of course, translated itself into increased respect for and confidence in the company, its products, sales representatives, and distributors.

This favorable recognition affected sales at all buying levels and in all markets. It paid off in other important respects, too, leading to favorable attitudes in the minds of legislators, national and community leaders, employees and prospective employees, stockholders and potential investors, and suppliers.

Extraordinary Response

Especially impressive was the extraordinary response from IP's own salespeople. Reports Richard J. Wiechmann:

> They called, they wrote, they personally buttonholed me to tell how the advertising opened doors for them—how it had been the factor that literally tipped orders in our favor. Eighty-five percent said their customers or prospects had commented on this campaign; 96 percent considered it helpful; 71 percent attributed inquiries or orders to it.
>
> By the tremendous demand for reprints of this advertising, we knew that the message in these ads had struck a responsive chord with millions of Americans. And we also knew, of course, that it was good business for us.

A CHANGING COMPANY

In 1960, IP was the world's leading supplier of paper for books, magazines, newspapers, and commercial printing, taken as a single category. The "Send me a man who reads!" campaign, promoting the value, enjoyment, and rewards of reading, was totally on target for the kind of product sales support IP required. But by the 1970s the picture had changed.

The company had developed the packaging side of its business to the point where IP was now the world's leading paper packaging company. Wood products had also grown, with the company ranking fourth in lumber production and sixth in plywood. Other investments—including an oil company—led management to believe that IP might be a "land resources management company." It just wasn't the same company anymore.

Special campaigns were prepared to address these issues individually, but with a resulting confusion of image. One frustrated publishing customer echoed the concern of his peers when he asked: "Are you guys still a *paper* company?" You know you're in trouble when one of your most important group of customers questions your commitment to its business.

DEMONSTRATING A COMMITMENT

The following is a quote from Robert Lauterborn, then director of marketing communications at IP:

Courtesy of International Paper.

Courtesy of International Paper.

There were a lot of ways we might have addressed this problem. For example, we could have run a series of ads in *Editor & Publisher, Folio, High Volume Printing* and so forth saying "IP is committed to the printing and publishing industry."

This would have been true, of course, but frankly, I think that sort of thing is a waste of time and a waste of money. Hardly anyone reads that sort of thing, and nobody believes it.

What we did decide to do was what all good advertising does—*demonstrate* the point it wants to make.

International Paper sought to *prove* it was committed to the publishing business by dealing directly with one of their customers' most nagging long-term concerns: the ability and propensity of young people to read and write as well as they must in order to be able to cope in this age of increasing competition.

Lauterborn continues:

Again, there were various ways we might have addressed the issue. We might have pointed with alarm at the apparent problem. We could have put together an ad that said "Look at these declining SAT verbal scores." And in truth that might have accomplished the purpose.

Such a campaign would have produced all kinds of letters saying "Boy, IP, you've really put your finger on the problem." But that's a demagogue's solution—point with alarm but do nothing to solve the problem.

Actually the SAT scores showed something quite different from what is generally supposed. They showed a *positive* story for print, not a negative one. With as many as 50 percent of high school students going on to higher education, declining test scores indicated, to some degree, the inclusion of a great many more people in the American dream—and a huge increase in the demographics which most favor print.

Market Development: 1990

International Paper felt that what it should really do was help publishers realize that potential. Research showed that young people were actually far more interested in the basic skills of reading and writing than was popularly supposed. And they needed help in developing the level of communications skills that life demands in an information-rich society.

International Paper decided to try to provide some of that help, to actually help young people read, write, and communicate better. The belief was that if they could read and write better they would read and write more. Then customers would sell more books, magazines, and newspapers, and IP would sell more paper.

The target audience selected was young people aged 15–30: high school students on their way to college, current college students, and recent college graduates. This group was projected to be the heaviest readers of books, magazines, and newspapers ten years down the road. In the 1980s this population segment would grow at a rate four times that of the U.S. population as a whole. What IP was really doing was ''1990 market development'' for its customers.

Power of the Printed Word

Over the course of several months, IP's agency, Ogilvy & Mather, produced seven different creative approaches. The idea finally selected employed a series of black-and-white, two-page spreads, each focusing on some different aspect of written communication. Each was bylined by a celebrity knowledgeable in the field. (See illustrations.)

The campaign was to be known as ''The Power of the Printed Word,'' and included:

''How to read faster'' by Bill Cosby

''How to write a business letter'' by Malcolm Forbes

''How to improve your vocabulary'' by Tony Randall

''How to write clearly'' by Edward Thompson

''How to write with style'' by Kurt Vonnegut

''How to use a library'' by James Michener

''How to enjoy the classics'' by Steve Allen

''How to read an annual report'' by Jane Bryant Quinn

''How to make a speech'' by George Plimpton

''How to write a resume'' by Dr. Jerrold Simon

''How to enjoy poetry'' by James Dickey

''How to spell'' by John Irving

''How to punctuate'' by Russell Baker

''How to encourage your child to read'' by Erma Bombeck

''How to read a newspaper'' by Walter Cronkite

''How to write a personal letter'' by Garrison Keillor

Virtually the entire media budget was allocated to reaching the target audience, with International Paper depending on merchandising to carry the message to their printing and publishing customers.

How to write a personal letter

by Garrison Keillor

International Paper asked Garrison Keillor, author of the best-selling books, Happy to Be Here and Lake Wobegon Days, to tell you how to write a letter that will bring joy into the life of someone you love.

We shy persons need to write a letter now and then, or else we'll dry up and blow away. It's true. And I speak as one who loves to reach for the phone, dial the number, and talk. I say, "Big Bopper here— what's shakin', babes?" The telephone is to shyness what Hawaii is to February, it's a way out of the woods, and yet: a letter is better.

Such a sweet gift

Such a sweet gift—a piece of handmade writing, in an envelope that is not a bill, sitting in our friend's path when she trudges home from a long day spent among wahoos and savages, a day our words will help repair. They don't need to be immortal, just sincere. She can read them twice and again tomorrow: You're someone I care about, Corinne, and think of often

and every time I do you make me smile.

We need to write, otherwise nobody will know who we are. They will have only a vague impression of us as A Nice Person, because frankly, we don't shine at conversation, we lack the confidence to thrust our faces forward and say, "Hi, I'm Heather Hooten, let me tell you about my week." Mostly we say "Uh-huh" and "Oh really." People smile and look over our shoulder, looking for someone else to talk to.

So a shy person sits down and writes a letter. To be known by another person—to meet and talk freely on the page—to be close despite distance. To escape from anonymity and be our own sweet selves and express the music of our souls.

Same thing that moves a giant rock star to sing his heart out in front of 123,000 people moves us to take ballpoint in hand and write a few lines to our dear Aunt Eleanor. We want to be known. We want her to know that we have fallen in love, that we quit our job, that we're moving to New York, and we want to say a few things that might not get said in casual conversation: thank you for what you've meant to me. I am very happy right now.

Skip the guilt

The first step in writing letters is to get over the guilt of not writing. You don't "owe" anybody a letter. Letters are a gift. The burning shame you feel when you see unanswered mail makes it harder to pick up a pen and makes for a cheerless letter when you finally do. I feel bad about not writing, but I've been so busy, etc. Skip this. Few letters are obligatory, and they are Thanks for the wonderful gift and I am terribly sorry to hear about George's death and Yes, you're welcome to stay with us next month, and not many more than that. Write those promptly if you want to keep your friends. Don't worry about the others, except love letters, of course. When your true love writes Dear Light of My Life, Joy of My Heart, O Lovely Pulsating Core of My Sensate Life, some response is called for.

Some of the best letters are tossed off in a burst of inspiration, so keep your writing stuff in one place where you can sit down for a few minutes and Dear Roy,

"If you like to receive mail as much as I do, here's one infallible rule: To get a letter, you've got to send a letter."

Courtesy of International Paper.

I am in the middle of an essay for International Paper but thought I'd drop you a line. Hi to your sweetie too dash off a note to a pal. Envelopes, stamps, address book, everything in a drawer so you can write fast when the pen is hot.

A blank white 8" x 11" sheet can look as big as Montana if the pen's not so hot—try a smaller page and write boldly. Or use a note card with a piece of fine art on the front; if your letter ain't good, at least they get the Matisse. Get a pen that makes a sensuous line, get a comfortable typewriter, a friendly word processor—whichever feels easy to the hand.

Sit for a few minutes with the blank sheet in front of you, and meditate on the person you will write to, let your friend come to mind until you can almost see her or him in the room with you. Remember the last time you saw each other and how your friend looked and what you said and what perhaps was unsaid between you, and when your friend becomes real to you, start to write.

Tell us what you're doing

Write the salutation—*Dear You* —and take a deep breath and plunge in. A simple declarative sentence will do, followed by another and another and another. Tell us what you're doing and tell it like you were talking to us. Don't think about grammar, don't think about lit'ry style, don't try to write dramatically, just give us your news. Where did you go, who did you see, what did they say, what do you think?

If you don't know where to begin, start with the present mo-ment: I'm sitting at the kitchen table on a rainy Saturday morning. Everyone is gone and the house is quiet. Let your simple description of the present moment lead to something else, let the letter drift gently along.

Take it easy

The toughest letter to crank out is one that is meant to impress, as we all know from writing job applications; if it's hard work to slip off a letter to a friend, maybe you're trying too hard to be terrific. A letter is only a report to someone who already likes you for reasons other than your brilliance. Take it easy.

Don't worry about form. It's not a term paper. When you come to the end of one episode, just start a new paragraph. You can go from a few lines about the sad state of rock 'n roll to the fight with your mother to your fond memories of Mexico to your cat's urinary tract infection to a few thoughts on personal indebtedness to the kitchen sink and what's in it. The more you write, the easier it gets, and when you have a True True Friend to write to, a *compadre*, a soul sibling, then it's like driving a car down a country road, you just get behind the keyboard and press on the gas.

Don't tear up the page and start over when you write a bad line— try to write your way out of it. Make mistakes and plunge on. Let the letter cook along and let yourself be bold. Outrage, confusion, love—whatever is in your mind, let it find a way to the page. Writing is a means of discovery, always, and when you come to the end and write *Yours ever* or *Hugs and Kisses*, you'll know something you didn't when you wrote *Dear Pal*.

An object of art

Probably your friend will put your letter away, and it'll be read again a few years from now— and it will improve with age. And forty years from now, your friend's grandkids will dig it out of the attic and read it, a sweet and precious relic of the ancient Eighties that gives them a sudden clear glimpse of you and her and the world we old-timers knew. You will then have created an object of art. Your simple lines about where you went, who you saw, what they said, will speak to those children and they will feel in their hearts the humanity of our times.

You can't pick up a phone and call the future and tell them about our times. You have to pick up a piece of paper.

Garrison Keillor

"Outrage, confusion, love—whatever is in your mind, let it find a way to the page."

Would Young People Read the Ads?

The pieces had to have genuine educational validity, of course, and the celebrities had to be credible. However, the real and very key question was would young people actually read 1,500-word ads? Did they really care that much about the printed word? Says Lauterborn:

> We held our breath and tested the concept. We picked one northern and one southern city to see if there were regional differences. There weren't. We showed young people in each area mock-ups of the ads along with 21 author-title combinations.
>
> The response was overwhelming. Ninety-two percent of the high school students studied said they would read three or more of the pieces. More than two-thirds said they would read seven or more. Eighty-six percent of college students said they would read three or more, as did 77 percent of recent college graduates.

Teachers also were surveyed to see if they had any objections to the concept. They didn't. In fact they were unanimously enthusiastic and even made an important contribution to the program. They asked for teaching guides to help them use the pieces in their classrooms. International Paper contracted with *Scholastic* magazine to produce the guides and included them with all requests with school return addresses.

The campaign appeared in such publications as *Newsweek, People, Time* (College Edition), *Omni, Scholastic, Psychology Today, Ebony, New York Times School Weekly,* and even *Rolling Stone.* Selected pieces also ran in *Times' Science Times,* the *Wall Street Journal,* and other newspapers and specialized magazines.

The Flexibility to Fine-Tune

Important was the decision to use print—and not only because IP's customers were publishers and printers. Print allows readers to participate at their own pace, in their own time, wherever they may be. And with only a million or so dollars in the budget, print was certainly the most cost-effective way for the company to go.

Not to be overlooked is that print provided the flexibility for IP to fine-tune the schedule, exposing individual pieces to subgroups. "How to Read an Annual Report," for example, ran in *Barron's, Forbes, Fortune,* and the *Wall Street Journal* to reach a broader business and financial audience.

A High-Class Problem

Did the research hold up? Were the ads read? Well, as of early 1988, the company had received anywhere from 500 to 1,000 letters a *day* since the program began in 1982, with more than 30 million reprints sent out in response. For the first six months of the program IP had what they referred to as "a high-class problem"—fulfillment costs were running *10 times* budget.

There were more than 5,000 press pickups, and more than 2,000 companies, colleges, or other organizations reprinted one or more of the pieces. It was commended by publishers' associations, printers' groups, and educators. A telephone survey of 50 high school English teachers chosen at random around the country showed that all 50 were aware of the program and 47 were actually using it.

The campaign won many major awards—from the One Show for copy to the Art Directors Club Award and even the Public Relations Society of America (PRSA) Silver Anvil. And in 1983 it won the prestigious Stephen E. Kelly Award for the best magazine advertising campaign of the year.

"The Power of the Printed Word" has reached far beyond the original target audience. It was used from nursery schools to senior citizens' homes; in libraries, churches, prisons; with gifted students as well as with slow learners. It had tremendous impact in plant and mill communities and improved IP's college recruiting efforts.

THE BEST KIND OF RESPONSE ADVERTISING

It was successful because, as Lauterborn says, "it respected the reader's intelligence. It was the best kind of response advertising, because it set up a dialogue with the reader. It invited him to participate. I think that's much more effective than telling the reader what to think or preaching at him.

"This all too often produces one of two reactions: 'Ho-Hum' or 'Says who?' That's especially true when you're talking to students, who are very quick to turn you off or react negatively if you talk to them the wrong way."

The campaign was merchandised extensively and successfully in print by segmenting the audience and developing a rifle-shot creative and media approach. A one-page ad in college media positioned the series as a "College Survival Kit," extending the reach among college students. Of a similar nature were the "Athlete's Survival Kit" and an "Engineer's Survival Kit," each in the appropriate media.

So the students and their teachers liked the advertising. But how about IP's *customers?*

There's no question that publishers valued the program. They certainly gave it an extraordinary amount of merchandising support. The publisher of *Book Digest* wrote a publisher-to-publisher letter to 2,000 book publishers calling their attention to the program. The *New York Times* published its own set of teaching guides, using the newspaper to illustrate all the ads. And Doubleday made the series into a best-selling book, further extending "The Power of the Printed Word." And these are just a few examples.

The Inseparable Duo

During the almost 10 years the campaign ran, studies showed International Paper as the only paper company to gain appreciably in image. While competitors were being criticized on environmental issues, IP was being praised for its public service. The real proof of the pudding, however, is that during this time IP held on to important market share. And this despite their inability to make needed major capital investments or to offer any product advantage over competition. In fact, as business grew, IP was the first paper company to go on allocation, the last to come off.

Leo Burnett said: "Advertising communicates more than we intend." Who can measure what additional benefits "The Power of the Printed Word" may have supplied—what it may have meant to employee morale, to customers for other IP products, or to potential shareholders? As the Japanese put it: "One thing is said, and 10 things are understood."

The Japanese couldn't be more on target! There's no question but your company's image—be it good or bad—contributes to more than one aspect of your business. No matter what the primary objective of your image campaign, these ads often bear heavily on the sales, or lack of sales, of your product.

The subtitle of this chapter could be "Image and Brand: The Dynamic Duo." Or perhaps it should be: "The Inseparable Duo," because it's just about impossible to divorce a familiar and respected image from the successful sale of your product. Conversely, if your customers have little awareness of your company or a negative perspective, sales may be hard to come by.

Northwestern Mutual: "The Quiet Company"

Northwestern Mutual Life Insurance was one such company with surprisingly low awareness. Although the company had been in business successfully for more than 100 years, a Gallup study in the 1970s showed that Northwestern Mutual ranked only 34th in awareness with the general public from among the 55 largest life insurance companies. They were virtually unknown by their target market of well-educated, affluent adults, 25–54 years old.

Company advertising up to that time, such advertising as there was, had not been doing the job. After reviewing the Gallup findings, management agreed that Northwestern Mutual should mount a corporate campaign. They assigned three missions to this advertising.

First, they wanted advertising that would pre-sell the market, reducing the cost of selling and helping to recruit agents by the increased awareness. Next, the company looked to reinforce policy owner loyalty. Finally they sought to "energize" their distribution system by building pride and enthusiasm among their agents and employees.

It was decided that television would be the quickest and most efficient way of putting Northwestern Mutual on the map. Their first TV buy made them a 1/16 sponsor of the 1972 Olympics and the experience was dramatically rewarding. Awareness measurements after the telecasts boosted Northwestern Mutual to third place from thirty-fourth. They have been a TV "event" buyer, e.g., Olympics, Super Bowl, an occasional miniseries, ever since. Limited print support—on about a 70/30 basis—was added in 1980.

The creative theme had come quite naturally. In both formal research and informal conversations with the public, one question seemed to be repeated over and over: "If you're so good and have been around for more than 100 years, how come we've never heard of you?" The obvious answer: "Because we're the quiet company." And "The Quiet Company" became their signature and still is.

It has proved a most effective communications tool. Says John Caspari, director of advertising, "When we ask 'What does the quiet company mean?' they say, 'Oh, it means you're financially sound . . . you have high quality agents . . . your products are good'—all the good things! It certainly has been valuable in establishing the personality of our company as one of highest quality. We track the campaign at least twice a year, and have always been in the top ten since initiating the program."

Company agents are more than enthusiastic. Many of the general agents take advantage of the available co-op program and localize the national advertising to their own use. It not only supports their line of product, but it aids recruitment as well. Concludes Caspari, "Our co-op program is good for the agent, and it's good for us. In fact, we think these local versions probably work better than the national ads."

The Eaton Corporation Image Campaign

Eaton Corporation also understands the multi-mission concept. Their corporate advertising is designed with as many as four major goals in mind, and product marketing is an important one.

Courtesy of Northwestern Mutual Life Insurance Co.

Their corporate image campaign started, as so many do, with research. In the case of Eaton, a corporate reputation study had been conducted early in 1985 by Yankelovich, Skelly and White. The purpose of the study was to determine how Eaton was perceived by its business constituents, i.e., customers, suppliers, competitors, and business peers. A total of 206 executives from those groups were surveyed.

In addition, Eaton sought the opinions of 201 individuals in the financial community, including security analysts, portfolio managers, and retail brokers. The third major constituency measured was 179 Eaton shareholders, along with 183 individual investors who did not own the corporation's stock. With all groups, Eaton measured their image against those of five other companies so that results could be viewed with perspective.

The study showed that both the security analysts and the Eaton shareholders were very familiar with the company and gave it high ratings. This was not surprising as since 1980 Eaton had concentrated their communications efforts on those two audiences.

With the rest of their major constituents, however, the report was ''unflattering and disturbing.''

Their own customers said that they knew more about some of the other companies than they did about Eaton, and regarded the others more highly than Eaton. Less than 50 percent of the executives polled from customer companies felt they knew Eaton's operations well. That figure had been 71 percent in 1979. They also viewed Eaton less favorably than in 1979, and generally less favorably than the comparative companies.

AWARENESS BUT NOT FAMILIARITY

Most corporations have certain strengths they can call upon in difficult situations, and Eaton was no exception.

Even though the research indicated that their familiarity was relatively low, the Eaton name was known. There may not have been ''familiarity'' but there was ''awareness.''

Generally as the familiarity of your company increases, attitudes of target groups improve. This was dramatically the case with Eaton. The favorable research results from their shareholders and stock analysts were literally off the chart.

While there was a relative absence of strong positives in Eaton's image, there were no significant negatives to overcome. Eaton faced an immense communications challenge, but they also had a tremendous opportunity to build a powerful image on the basis of their achievements and future prospects.

Three Basic Functions

Remember, although it may have many missions, your corporate advertising has really only three basic functions.

1. Increase awareness.

2. Extend familiarity.

3. Influence attitudes.

They work in that order, too. In other words, if people have heard of you, and also have some notion of what it is you do and how it relates to them, you can attempt to influence their attitudes with some reasonable prospect of success.

The importance of increasing familiarity is to expand your audience's knowledge of your company from the one or two things they may already know to other things they may not know. This is significant because, as research shows, people who feel they know a company well are five times more likely to have a favorable opinion of that company than those who have little familiarity.

Four Corporate Objectives

Eaton understood this. From a recent presentation by Dennis A. Ritzel, director of advertising and corporate identity: "Our corporate image advertising program was developed with (those) three basic functions in mind and on the basis of the following four objectives:

1. Increase awareness of Eaton as a company successfully expanding from its leadership position in traditional markets to high-technology growth markets.

2. Support marketing efforts by enhancing Eaton's reputation as a company which produces innovative products for the markets it serves.

3. Increase the perception of the company's commitment to quality and customer satisfaction.

4. Establish a basis for a higher stock value by achieving broader recognition of Eaton's clearly defined business strategy, strong financial condition, and commitment to research and development.

"This was our 'response statement' . . . the response our ads would be designed to invoke: Eaton is an innovative and creative manufacturing company I should consider investing in or doing business with."

How Do You Show the Future *Today?*

How do you find the one creative strategy that will best establish your company as an innovative, future-oriented operation, with involvement and growth in a diverse range of industries? And, in Eaton's case, a strategy that would address the problem of basic identity weaknesses? Ritzel notes:

> Our constituents are thoughtful, intelligent leaders. We devised a creative approach that would respect their status, present our credentials in a visually bold way, and recognize the value of their time.
>
> "Future-oriented" might suggest the use of computer graphics or some other exotic technique, but we felt their use had been overworked and was more effective on television anyway. We were recommending a print-only campaign.
>
> We decided to use something else to represent the future—the universal and eternal surrogate for the future: children. Single word headlines would point up key corporate messages, with minimal copy to encourage readership. [See illustrations]

The first ad was headlined: "Diversification." The copy read: "Getting into new things. Because the future belongs to those who anticipate change—to Eaton."

A photo of a tomboy, with ballet shoes draped around her baseball bat, represents the fact that Eaton is a diversified company. Underneath the logo there is a tag line: "Growing into the future." There's also a listing of Eaton's four major business areas—Automotive, Electronics, Defense, Capital Goods.

Other ads—each with a child as surrogate for Eaton's future—are headed: "Transportation," "Electronics," "Avionics," and "Planning."

Obviously not every campaign can feature children. The lesson to be learned is that you can successfully create visual drama and interest by using a carefully chosen symbol to represent your company or some intangible characteristic of your company. And although long copy is often read thoroughly—International Paper is one good example—short copy is inviting, especially to the busy executive.

Eaton's ads were prepared in both one-page and two-page color versions and in black-and-white for newspapers. They were placed in suitable media to reach and influence a business community universe of about four million customers and potential customers in U.S. manufacturing firms and government, and about two million professionals in the financial area.

Courtesy of Eaton Corporation.

Courtesy of Eaton Corporation.

Courtesy of Eaton Corporation.

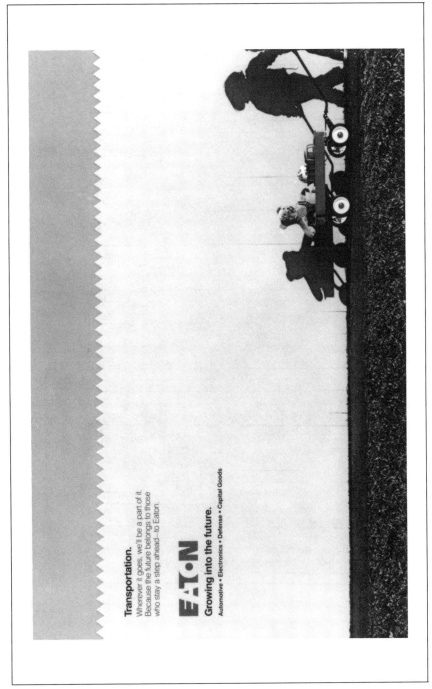

Courtesy of Eaton Corporation.

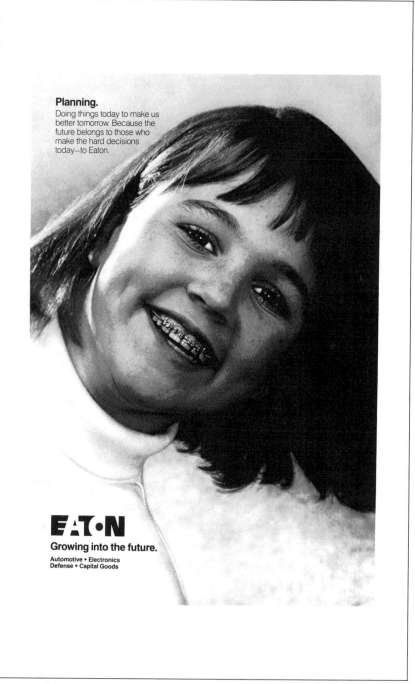

Courtesy of Eaton Corporation.

Setting the Stage for Product Advertising

Of particular significance, says Ritzel, "We invested about 11 percent of our total budget in trade magazines important to Eaton. We have the firm belief that corporate advertising and product advertising can reinforce and complement each other."

That is exactly what this chapter is all about. Whatever other purpose an image campaign may have, such advertising can almost always help prepare the marketplace for the sale of the product.

Look again at how some companies have used image advertising in this manner. Is there an application for your own business?

- Nabisco's use of a strong, positive corporate identity to tie diverse brands together . . . and make sales.
- Goodyear's image ads that maintained awareness over a three-year purchase span . . . to bring the customer back.
- Amoco's program to introduce a wide range of high-quality products to an ever-changing customer group . . . to educate and influence purchase choices.
- International Paper's need to demonstrate a commitment to worried customers . . . and keep them buying.
- Northwestern Mutual Life's use of what might be considered a negative attribute . . . to build a new market awareness.
- Eaton's successful attempt to regain a desired familiarity with key audiences . . . supporting marketing efforts, among other important objectives.

Whatever other goals they may have had, each company had its own good reasons to use image advertising to support product sales.

CHAPTER FIVE

Impacting the Financial Community:
Changing Investor Expectations

■ It's an unusual company, and a shortsighted one, that is not concerned with the image it presents to its shareholders and the rest of the financial world. Perceptions of a corporation by investors, stock analysts, portfolio managers, and brokers tend to affect a company's basic market value.

The primary job of management, of course, is to increase the corporation's value and thereby the wealth of its shareholders. Management achieves this by raising and budgeting capital for various projects, products, and markets. Every company program contributes to or interferes with this objective to some degree, and image advertising is no exception.

Three Ways Image Impacts Valuation

That image advertising can actually affect the price of a corporation's stock is debated by some. Research, however, tends to support the belief that this form of advertising does indeed influence valuation in at least three ways.

According to Eugene P. Schonfeld, in a comprehensive study, corporate advertising influences market valuation by:

1. Preparing markets for the company's products or services, thus increasing sales revenue and reducing market risk.

2. Influencing markets, thus lowering costs and operating risk.

3. Changing the expectations of investors regarding future returns and risks, by providing them with information which better enables them to interpret financial performance when making their investment decisions.[1]

Schonfeld continues: "Changes in investor expectations are likely to lead to higher or lower valuation of the firm as investors change stock trading behavior. . . . Corporate advertising may be targeted at institutional and individual investors to change their expectations about risk and returns.

"In the financial markets, corporate advertising can help a firm compete for capital at favorable rates and realize full market value for its financial performance. W.R. Grace, Northwest Industries, and other firms have used it, with varying success, to achieve higher valuation. Corporate advertising is (also) used to build confidence in the corporation among lenders."

STOCK VALUE CAN CHANGE BY 4 PERCENT

How much will corporate advertising influence a company's stock price? Schonfeld claims that under average conditions—i.e., average corporate financial conditions, an average stock market situation, and an average advertising budget and campaign—a typical firm would get a 4 percent higher stock price than if the company spent nothing on corporate advertising.

In a study done for Bozell & Jacobs, Inc., Jaye S. Niefeld arrives at the same 4 percent figure. Writing in *Industrial Marketing* Niefeld says:

> More than half (55%) of the price of a company's stock is determined by its financial fundamentals . . . about 40%, by the "romance of the market"

---

[1]"Profits from Corporate Advertising Investments," Eugene P. Schonfeld, October 15, 1982.

. . . [while] corporate advertising accounts for 4% of the variance in price of a stock.

We were at first rather humbled by that finding. But if one relates that figure to the realities of the market, the reaction changes. Given about 1,560 corporations listed on the New York Stock Exchange (as of June 30, 1979), each with an average of 18.8 million shares outstanding at an average price of $31.08 per share, the market value [*not* book value] of each company would average $584 million. A 4% variance in price would mean $1.24 per share— a potential incremental increase in market value to shareholders of more than $23 million per company with corporate advertising.

Since the average investment in corporate advertising of the companies studied was about $700,000, those figures could be interpreted as a 33 to 1 return on investment.[2]

Unfortunately, the Bozell & Jacobs study has never been repeated. It is reasonable to believe, however, that comparable statistics might be developed today, despite the many obvious economic changes that have taken place.

Success Depends upon Four Factors

These findings indicate that corporate image advertising can have a statistically significant relationship to stock price. Even so, success is not guaranteed. Advertising strategy and creative quality along with the market situation and timing are crucial.

Schonfeld puts it this way: "Effectiveness of a corporate campaign seems to depend on four critical factors: (1) the firm's current financial condition and trends, (2) the firm's position in the stock market, (3) the characteristics of the corporate advertising campaign used, and (4) the overall direction of the stock market.

"When conditions are 'right' and the campaign is 'right,' a firm may achieve results which are substantially above average."[3]

KNOW YOUR AUDIENCE

Every mission of image advertising has its own strategic and creative needs. The campaign that prepares the marketplace for a particular brand may take a totally different direction from the one announcing a corporate name change,

---

[2] "Corporate Advertising," Jaye S. Niefeld, *Industrial Marketing,* July, 1980.

[3] Schonfeld.

which, in turn, can vary dramatically from a campaign aimed at influencing government legislation.

When impacting the financial community it's vital to know and understand your audience. Stock analysts and brokers, shareholders and potential investors, bankers, and other lenders all need to know the hard financial facts of a corporation.

Susan Thomases, an attorney with New York City's Willkie Farr & Gallagher, comments: "The cornerstones of any program for investor relations are disclosure and communication. CEOs must learn to disclose even bad news. This builds shareholder trust by creating the impression that the corporation has nothing to hide.

"It's not product trust I'm talking about, but a kind of trust that focuses on what's in it for the shareholder and why he should stick with you in hard times. Thus the disclosure can assist in keeping the stock price up, and encourage the shareholder to support corporate strategy."

But besides hard financial facts, the shareholders need to know corporate policies, plans, and product developments—the kind of facts they cannot learn from electronic quotation systems and statements of condition. They often look to advertising as an important source of this information.

Determine Mission and Targets

As we saw in Chapter 3, the merger of the Chessie System Railroads and Seaboard Coast Line Industries resulted in a brand new and almost totally unknown corporation, CSX. It was the largest transportation and natural resource company in the nation. But nobody knew it, including most of the financial community.

CSX Chairman, Hays Watkins writes: "Early on we determined our CSX mission to be the leader in [the transportation and natural resource] field . . . to become known in the financial and investing communities . . . We think corporate advertising is an important tool in acquisitions and divestitures. The better known we are, the better position we're in.

"We're also convinced that our corporate advertising has an influence on our stock price . . . is a good long-term investment . . . not something you turn off to save money or turn on when you have an extra dollar."[4]

Writing in *Crosscurrents,* CSX spokesman, Edwin E. Edel, says: "One of our first moves was to find out what, if anything, the financial community—our key target audience—knew of CSX.

---

[4]"Parables for Peers," Hays Watkins, *Business Week* brochure, 1985.

"Benchmark studies . . . told us that while 44% of the specialized financial publics were aware of CSX, only 61% of the 44% knew that CSX was primarily a rail-holding company. The fact was that 95% of CSX revenues of some $5 billion were derived from its railroad operations."[5]

How CSX Showcased Its Strength and Potential

The first full-color spread (see illustration) established the CSX look. A striking visual of shiny steel rails running into the sun announces a new day. The CSX name is displayed boldly as a headline, with a subhead proclaiming: "The New Number One." The CSX name was repeated prominently in the logo, grouped with those of Chessie and Seaboard. Various other CSX holdings were listed across the bottom of the ad.

Ads appeared in national business and financial publications, and two eight-week flights of TV commercials appeared on selected news shows on the three networks at approximately 50 GRPs a week.

All ads displayed the corporate name dramatically and featured eye-catching visuals tied in directly to CSX operations. Impact on targets was strong and direct: CSX Corporation must be a major factor in the railroad business.

CSX had set an awareness goal of 67 percent for the first six months. This was a 50 percent increase over the 44 percent figure of the original benchmarks. When the campaign had run for five months, a follow-up study was conducted. Now the awareness level had increased to 84 percent, and the understanding of CSX had grown from 60 percent to 93 percent.

Eventually the advertising emphasis changed from just promoting the CSX name to giving the reader more information about the new corporation: specifically that CSX was a state-of-the-art, computer-controlled transportation system. Just beneath the logo was a brand new position line: "American's Largest Transportation and Natural Resource Company."

TWO CRITICAL WORDS

From almost the beginning, in addition to advertising to financial and business publics, CSX used its advertising to support the marketing of subsidiary companies. CSX was able to use most of their corporate ads in freight publications

---

[5]"The Joy of CSX," Edwin E. Edel, *Crosscurrents,* Vol. 12, 1983.

Courtesy of the CSX Corporation.

as well. This gave important continuity to the look of their advertising, more mileage for their ad dollars. Naturally copy was rewritten for shippers and had a more hard-selling tone. A freight theme line was added, too: "Single-System Service throughout the Eastern Half of the USA."

Concludes corporate spokesman Edel: "If there are two words I would hope you remember, they are: *research*—it's critical to the success of any advertising program—and *continuity*—you must have a program for the long pull and not keep changing for change's sake. . . ."[6] This is surely one lesson to take to heart. Research can tell you where you are, help you see where you need to go, while continuity allows the strategies chosen to get you there to have a chance to work.

Harry O'Neill, of Opinion Research Corporation, has said:

> The research behind the corporate campaign has its purpose in providing you with intelligence on how business, your industry, and your company stand in the eyes of those publics important to you. This intelligence . . . should be gathered systematically and on a continuous basis.
>
> The best research behind the best corporate campaign is not enough. There remains one final and all-important area of communication—your company's performance.
>
> A good financial-communications program is [no] substitute for sound financial performance. All things being equal, however, the company with a balanced, sophisticated communications program stands a much better chance of gaining the financial world's attention than does the company that assumes that financial performance will necessarily speak for itself."[7]

Print Media: A Cost-effective Road to Familiarity

Unlike CSX, Eaton opted for a print campaign only. They knew that television was an exciting medium, certainly superb for building awareness. However, Eaton felt that when trying to improve corporate familiarity with relatively small segments of the public, TV was not cost effective. But print media was.

---

[6]Edel.

[7]"The Research Behind a Corporate Campaign," Harry O'Neill, *Crosscurrents, Vol. 7, 1978.*

Eaton's campaign had a successful two-year run. Later benchmarks indicated that goals had been reached, that the company's image with key audiences was strengthened. Eaton had painted a picture of its own future, and investors and customers liked what they saw. Did it increase stock price substantially? Possibly not. But it *did* bring the company's true worth to the attention of many influential financial professionals.

When Perceptions Can't Keep Pace with Realities

CSX had the problem of introducing what, in effect, was a brand new corporation, and Eaton needed to redefine what had become almost an unknown corporation. In Allied-Signal's case, however, the assignment was to unravel a rather confused corporate image—a "loused-up identity" as one spokesperson put it—to give investors and others in the financial spectrum a clearer picture of the company's move into the high-tech marketplace.

For starters, the corporation had had three different names in less than nine years. As Allied Chemical, its image was that of a stodgy commodity chemicals supplier. Its next identity, Allied Corp., did little if anything to alter the picture. The last version, Allied Signal Corp., reflects its major corporate component origins, Allied Corporation, and the Signal Companies, a diversified technology company based in La Jolla, California.

In adopting that name, the corporation sought to establish a high-technology reputation, one that would point to the dramatic changes it had undergone as it moved from commodity chemicals, oil and gas, to specialty chemicals, fibers, and engineered materials, primarily serving the aerospace, electronics, and automotive industries.

"Our objective is to demonstrate how Allied-Signal has become a progressive, high-technology company, to influential audiences who may not know the full scope of our capabilities," explained David G. Powell, senior vice president for public affairs, writing in *Omnia,* the company's quarterly magazine. "Allied-Signal has undergone a major transformation, and outside perceptions simply haven't kept pace with realities."[8]

---

[8]"Powerful Persuaders," David G. Powell, *Omnia,* Winter 1986.

AGENCY BEGINS WITH RESEARCH

The agency selected for the advertising part of the image communications program, Homer & Durham Advertising Ltd., began their assignment with four months of intensive research on several levels. They visited Allied-Signal locations nationwide and interviewed numerous managers and executives, including Chairman Ed Hennessy, to gain a firsthand understanding of the company's major strengths.

The agency also took an "intelligence inventory," both of what was known by key groups and of what was *not* known, with emphasis on the business and financial publics.

The result was a series of strong, attention-demanding ads, consistent in appearance and unlike the usual run-of-the-mill corporate ads. Respecting the average reader's tight schedule and lack of reading time, Homer & Durham created ads with striking photography, terse copy, and direct, single-word headlines: *technology, benefit, future,* etc. The format was not unlike Eaton's, but with a totally different photographic direction.

Designed to be compatible with Allied-Signal's product ads in trade publications, the image series emphasized the company's role as a leader in technology, leaving the marketing ads to focus on individual product performance and reliability. In all of the image ads, there was repeated mention of appropriate Allied-Signal businesses or products, based on the technology being featured.

"Not the Old Allied Chemical"

Exploratory research tested the campaign's effectiveness with target audiences. Results were more than encouraging. Interviews were conducted with professional portfolio managers and individual investors. Among private investors the ads produced striking changes in perceptions of Allied-Signal. Messages were thought to be positive and visuals eye-catching.

"This is not the old Allied Chemical I knew,"[9] commented one typical investor.

Financial professionals, too, learned something new about the company. They recognized that Allied-Signal was changing its direction through the addition of new technologies, companies, and products, and they thought the ads were "a plus for further investment." Declared a broker, "I'll take a fresh look at the company."

A final word from Powell: "Getting people to understand who we really are and the breadth of our technological capabilities won't be accomplished overnight, but this program [helps]."

---

[9]Powell.

Courtesy of Allied-Signal Inc.

How United Technologies Built Their Image

Like Allied-Signal, United Technologies Corporation was a new, and largely unfamiliar, corporate name. A good part of its problem originated with the company's name change from United Aircraft Corporation in 1975. But it was also because there were no products carrying the corporate identity. There was no way to promote the name effectively in the course of daily business.

United Technologies did have one important advantage. The names of its major divisions and subsidiaries were very well known in their own right. Brands like Carrier, Otis, Pratt & Whitney, and Sikorsky were leaders in their respective fields. They had impressive identities of their own—identities that could be employed to build familiarity for the parent company.

The corporation reasoned that the more investors recognized the United Technologies name and tied it to the successes of its divisions, the greater respect the company would receive in the investing community. Higher market valuation was expected to follow.

Corporate image advertising was not unfamiliar to United Technologies. They were already running a series of monthly, all-type ads in the *Wall Street Journal*. In these the corporation commented on timely, topical issues and invited readers to send for reprints. (See illustrations.) Response was staggering. By the time this landmark campaign ended in 1986, well over four million reprints had been sent out.

But now was the time to add a second image campaign to the mix. Gordon Bowman, then head of United Technologies' creative programs, didn't want merely to show products in this new campaign. By concentrating on the triumphs of its highly visible brands, Bowman sought to establish an image of a company on the cutting edge of many important projects—a company on the move in the high-tech world. He wanted advertising that would project corporate characteristics of innovation, high technology, and creative energy, but without using those actual words. He looked for strong visuals with simple, direct copy to explain to investors, financial professionals, and corporate heads the relationship between United Technologies and its divisions and subsidiaries.

Value Added by the "Halo Effect"

Certainly one of the purposes of this campaign was to make United Technologies better known to the investing and business communities through association with its strong brand images. But the company also looked for a "halo effect" from the advertising; this was the value added by the corporation to already successful brands. Says Thomas Haas, advertising manager, "Research showed that when people had an understanding of all that United Technologies was and could do, they had a better perception of individual units, even if they knew the units.

"It's rather trite, but the more you know us the more likely you are to favorably consider us."

More Editorial Than Advertising

The campaign's big, full-bleed, full-color spread format, with striking Jay Maisel photographs and brief, understated copy, looked more like editorial than advertising. (See illustrations.) Nor was there any official logo or signature to most of the ads. Center spread positions in *The New Yorker* and the *New York Times Magazine* (and later on *Time*'s 33 metro editions) was the perfect environment for reaching a majority of the target audiences.

The ads appeared monthly for almost seven years—a long run by almost any standard, and certainly an indication that management believed the series was doing the job, despite a lack of formal research measurement.

Senior vice president of corporate communications, Ray D'Argenio, felt the campaign definitely had impact, but that the impact had to be viewed as part of United Technologies total communications efforts. *"The Wall Street Journal* ads address individuals as human beings. The color spreads are in the magazines that these same people read on weekends. The two reinforce each other."[10]

Investment Community Buys the Future

More specifically, Thomas Haas notes:

> I feel that [corporate image advertising] supports the price of the stock. I don't believe you can expect advertising to drive up the price of the stock, but it certainly supports it. You still have to have the underlying value in the marketplace.
>
> We've talked to analysts and [they say] they're not swayed by advertising. But they are well aware of it. They look at it to find the edge. They look at it to see: what kind of company is this? . . . how does it present itself? . . . are they saying the same things in their advertising as they're saying at the analysts meetings?
>
> Analysts also say things like: is there something coming across in the advertising that we may not be picking up—a change in business they're

---

[10]"The Big Bang Theory," Sid Karpoff, *Madison Avenue*, February, 1985.

A flying start.

You're looking at the busiest terminal in the world's busiest airport. United Airlines at O'Hare. 400 flights a day through 85 acres of terminal. That means a lot of escalators, moving walks and elevators. And no room for bottlenecking breakdowns. To handle all these millions of people smoothly and efficiently, United needed big and they needed good. Fortunately, there's a word for that in Chicago. Otis.

The companies of United Technologies are working together on technologies that get people where they're going. Otis elevates in more than 140 countries worldwide. Pratt & Whitney powers more jet airliners than anyone else. UT Automotive makes vital parts of nearly every car on the road. And our propulsion systems are behind the most exciting journey of all—the exploration of space.

UNITED TECHNOLOGIES

Courtesy of United Technologies Corporation.

Courtesy of United Technologies Corporation.

Courtesy of United Technologies Corporation.

not talking about? [Analysts and investors look] for all sorts of messages. The fact that your company is out there in the business and trade press and is a known entity helps a portfolio manager make his recommendations to his investment committee. In other words, it helps if you don't have to say: "What is United Technologies?"

Bowman puts it this way: "The investment community buys the future, not the present, and the qualities these ads suggest are the things the investor looks for and has to feel subliminally about a company."[11]

Missions May Change, but the Importance of Image Goes On

United Technologies ran the campaign for about eight years. In 1988 it moved on to another program—another color-spread series—but one that talks more about the company through its specific products, and one that emphasizes the many different resources the company can bring to bear on particular problems.

Formats and messages may change as corporations themselves change, and as management determines new missions for corporate advertising. But the need to present a favorable image to investors and other publics goes on.

Four individual approaches to a single mission—as individual as the corporations sponsoring them, but with several distinct similarities:

1. The use of major space (often spreads) in leading business and investor publications.

2. The use of dramatic (often symbolic) four-color photography.

3. The use of short, direct copy, often with one-word headlines.

4. A message that demonstrates that this corporation leads the way into the future with its capabilities, products, and achievements.

Is this a winning formula? For some it will be; for others, maybe not. So much depends on corporate goals, a campaign's consistency, and the quality and appropriateness of creative work. But whatever else, it is obviously a direct approach to a particular problem.

---

[11]"The Big Bang Theory."

CHAPTER SIX

Advocacy Advertising:
Presenting the Company's Position on Key Issues

■ Perhaps no form of advertising creates such controversy as so-called "advocacy" advertising, sometimes called issue or constituency advertising. Although it accounts for no more than 10 percent of total corporate ad spending, advocacy advertising, as no other, creates special attention, often even heated argument.

Some CEOs feel it their corporate duty to speak out on thorny public issues. They believe that the media distort or even ignore the business world's point of view. These advertisers back up their beliefs with their budgets, seeking to inform and motivate the right people at the right time on subjects of importance to the company. The "right" people, of course, may be anyone from the public in general to small segments of the public, such as key legislators and government officials. And paid advertising is an effective way to reach them.

What kind of subjects? Governmental policies and legislation affecting the company, its industry, or business in general make perfect grist for the mill. So, too, do social and environmental problems and other issues of broad interest.

Some observers are concerned, however, and oppose advocacy advertising because they fear an imbalance in the presentation of ideas. They see the possibility of giant corporations spending millions of dollars to unduly influence the public one way or another in matters of national importance.

At one point the controversy was so active that the American Association of Advertising Agencies (AAAA) felt it necessary to issue a brochure ("Advocacy Advertising," June 1980) clarifying their own position. Not surprisingly, they were for advocacy advertising, pointing out that it is fully protected by the First Amendment and presuming that the great majority of it will be "prepared responsibly, by responsible men and women."

What Is Advocacy Advertising?

In that same brochure, the AAAA proposed its definition of the term: "Advocacy advertising may be defined as advertising paid for by a corporation and designed to communicate the company's position on public issues which have some connection with its business activities. This definition would include, at one end of the spectrum, statements of position on pending legislation. It would exclude, at the other end, product advertising or corporate 'goodwill' advertising aimed at corporate name or product recognition."

We might add that advocacy advertising may also focus on issues that are not necessarily national or even connected to business activities.

Peace on Earth, Screaming, and John Wayne

In Chapter 5 we learned how United Technologies Corporation (UTC) based its image advertising for many years on the achievements of its well-known brands. UTC's initial corporate effort, however, was a form of advocacy advertising. This was an all-type series, appearing in the *Wall Street Journal,* especially designed to let the world know what *kind* of company United Technologies is. It was a series of messages discussing life in general rather than life at the corporation. And it did its job with extraordinary effect!

The campaign's theme was: How we perform as individuals will determine how we perform as a nation. Just a few of its more than 75 messages touched on such varied matters as: education, memos, failure, peace on earth, workmanship, kids, parents, meetings, patriotism, little things, screaming, and John Wayne. That the ads touched the heart as well as the mind is borne out by almost a million letters requesting more than four million reprints.

In his introduction to "Gray Matter," a published collection of these messages (see illustrations), Harry J. Gray, former UTC chairman, wrote:

> I don't know for sure why this series has been so astonishingly effective. But I have some theories.
>
> For one thing, I believe we were right to invite readers to think— instead of telling them how to think.
>
> I believe we did well to discuss everyday subjects that affect everyone in some way, instead of talking about ourselves.
>
> I think we were wise to stay with problems that can be solved rather than tackling complex, abstract problems that elude solution.
>
> Most basically, I believe we struck a responsive chord with (the campaign's theme) . . . Readers evidently find the theme sensible and inspiring at the same time.[1]

Was there anything especially controversial about this advertising? Not really. Most of us can relate personally and positively to the topics covered, and it's hard to argue against motherhood and apple pie. Does a lack of controversy inhibit advocacy advertising? Obviously not, judging from the heavy response the campaign generated.

Nevertheless, there are some classic and *highly* controversial advocacy campaigns to be studied.

Two Outstanding Campaigns from W.R. Grace & Co.

W.R. Grace & Co. has been a leading practitioner of advocacy advertising for a number of years. And one of the reasons the company turned to this form of image building is because its chairman and CEO, J. Peter Grace, got himself so totally and enthusiastically involved. Said one agency account man: "We consider Peter Grace to be our junior copywriter."[2]

---

[1]"Gray Matter," Harry J. Gray, United Technologies Corporation, 1986.

[2]"Speaking Out Can Be Good for Your Corporate Health," Barbara Mehlman, *Madison Avenue,* February 1983.

Let's Get Rid Of "The Girl"

Wouldn't 1979 be
a great year
to take one giant
step forward
for womankind
and get rid of
"the girl"?
Your attorney says,
"If I'm not here
just leave it with
the girl."
The purchasing agent
says, "Drop off your
bid with the girl."
A manager says,
"My girl will get
back to your girl."
What girl?
Do they mean
Miss Rose?
Do they mean
Ms. Torres?
Do they mean
Mrs. McCullough?
Do they mean
Joy Jackson?
"The girl"
is certainly
a woman when she's
out of her teens.
Like you,
she has a name.
Use it.

To The Kid On The End Of The Bench

Champions once sat
where you're sitting,
kid.
The Football Hall of Fame
(and every other Hall of Fame)
is filled with names of people
who sat, week after week,
without getting a spot of
mud on their well-laundered
uniforms.
Generals,
senators,
surgeons,
prize-winning novelists,
professors,
business executives
started on the end of
a bench, too.
Don't sit and study
your shoe tops.
Keep your eye on
the game.
Watch for defensive
lapses.
Look for offensive
opportunities.
If you don't think you're
in a great spot,
wait until you see how many
would like to take it away
from you at next spring
practice.
What you do from the bench
this season
could put you on the field
next season,
as a player,
or back in the grandstand
as a spectator.

Aim So High You'll Never Be Bored

The
greatest waste
of our
natural resources
is the
number of
people
who never
achieve their
potential.
Get out
of that
slow lane.
Shift
into that
fast lane.
If you think
you can't,
you won't.
If you think
you can,
there's a
good chance
you will.
Even making
the effort
will make
you feel
like a new
person.
Reputations
are made
by searching
for things that
can't be done
and doing them.
Aim low:
boring.
Aim high:
soaring.

© United Technologies Corporation, June 1981.

Peter Grace wet his feet in issue advertising during President Carter's administration. Carter was in favor of increasing the capital gains tax from 48 to 52 percent, and this was enough to get Grace moving into the advocacy advertising arena.

On the principle that the best defense is a strong offense, Grace's ads not only asked the president not to increase the capital gains tax, but even suggested that he *reduce* the tax to 25 percent. At the same time statistics were developed to support Peter Grace's contention that an increase in the capital gains tax would have a decidedly negative effect on the economy by reducing investments in business.

The statistics became the basis of a series of anti-tax-increase, editorial-style ads with such provocative headlines as: "The small investor: An endangered species" and "Taxes up. Productivity down. Could we be doing something wrong?" (See illustrations.) Ads ran initially in the *Wall Street Journal,* the *New York Times,* and the *Washington Post.* Eventually the campaign rolled out in papers across the country.

Results couldn't have been better. Says Stephen B. Elliott, then Grace's director of corporate advertising: "We spent $400,000 and the capital gains tax was reduced to 28 percent. Our ads had even been picked up in editorial in papers where we didn't advertise.

"The campaign opened up relations with Congress we never had before. Congressmen came to us with economic questions and wanted [Peter Grace's] opinion. Grace suddenly became an authority in Washington."[3]

Grace also became a confirmed believer in the ability of advocacy advertising to reach and influence the right people at the right time.

In Chapter 1 we saw how, in a subsequent campaign, W.R. Grace got extra mileage for its advertising dollar by tackling national issues in which the company "could be perceived as having enlightened self-interest as well as concern for the community and nation." This was merely a continuation of lessons learned in the fight against a higher capital gains tax.

The Grace ad we cited—the famous "baby" ad—focused on the national debt and what it means to each of us. But this was only one of a long series of powerful TV and print ads that called national attention not only to the federal debt but to such subjects as productivity, taxes, and the deficit.

Some of those ads raised eyebrows. From an interview with Antonio Navarro, Grace senior vice president: "In our productivity ad [see illustration], which showed the Tokyo Giants at bat, the whole idea was to say: Here are the Japanese doing a great job in productivity (as well as in baseball). We taught

---

[3]*Madison Avenue.*

The small investor: An endangered species.

You don't have to be a millionaire to have a stake in the capital gains tax debate.

Small investors – indeed, all Americans – will be directly affected by this issue. And it's quickly coming to a head.

On the one hand, there are those who favor proposals to reduce the maximum tax rate on capital gains.

The Administration, on the other hand, rejects these proposals, claiming they would bring windfall profits to the rich, while leaving the average American in the lurch.

But the facts are that nearly two-thirds of total capital gains are realized by individuals with adjusted gross incomes of *under $50,000.* At W.R. Grace & Co., it is precisely the small investor we want to support. The individual whose right to property is being threatened by inflation and taxes. Each of these investors would benefit from the proposals, and *all* Americans would share in the other economic benefits which would result from reduced capital gains taxes.

Consider the following:

- Over the past ten years, the U.S. economy has steadily deteriorated, as shown in the table below:

THE DETERIORATING U.S. ECONOMY (5 Years Ending in Year Shown)				% Deterioration 1968-1977
	1968	1973	1977	
Real GNP (Average Annual % Change)	4.8%	3.3%	2.7%	(43.8)%
Unemployment Rate (Average %)	4.2	5.0	6.7	(59.5)
Real Business Investment (Average Annual % Change)	8.0	3.9	1.7	(78.8)
Inflation (Average Annual % Change)	2.6	5.0	7.7	(196.2)
Federal Deficit (Average. $ Billions)	$(4.7)	$(9.9)	$(38.2)	(712.8)
Maximum Capital Gains Tax (Single Year Rate)	25.0%	45.0%	49.1%	(96.4)

- Reversing these economic trends will require vigorous and productive investment in American business.
- Yet, the combination of 50% capital gains tax and 7% inflation has made it exactly 2.4 to 3.1 times tougher now to realize the same real profit from an investment than it was in the mid-sixties.

- This increased investment risk has all but crushed the incentive to invest. So much so that individual participation in equity markets declined 26% between 1968 and 1976. Like an endangered species, the choice for the small investor has been: flight or fight. So far, he has fled.

A deteriorating economy affects every American, regardless of income level or tax status.

Our point is simple and obvious. The best way to stimulate investment – and hence the economy as a whole – is to reduce the taxes that are forcing investors to turn away from equity markets.

Some experts say that reducing the maximum capital gains tax rate to 25% would free billions of dollars for productive investment. Enough to create some 440,000 jobs. Enough, in fact, to add $16 billion to federal revenues by 1985.

If you, too, think the small investor is an "endangered species," we urge you to write the Chairman of the House Ways and Means Committee, the Chairman of the Senate Finance Committee, or your elected Senators and Representatives, and tell them to:

1. *Reduce the short-term capital gains tax to a maximum of 25% and, on a sliding scale, lower that tax rate to zero for assets held over 10 years.*

2. *Stop double taxation of dividends by excluding dividend income from federal taxation – at least to some reasonable annual amount, like $1,000 or $2,000 per taxpayer.*

3. *Stop the unprecedented government deficit spending which has become a major source of inflation.*

An economy which depends on private capital for growth can't afford to bite the hand that feeds it. And heavy taxes on investment dollars are doing just that.

Writing your Congressman to lower investor taxes is one way to make sure our economy continues to make sense.

One step ahead of a changing world.

GRACE
chemicals · natural resources · consumer products

W.R. Grace & Co., 1114 Avenue of the Americas, New York, N.Y. 10036

Courtesy of W. R. Grace & Co.

them 'the game,' and now they're beating us at it. Some Japanese . . . claimed our campaign was 'racist.' Well it patently was not, unless showing the Japanese as clever, innovative, productive, efficient, and, finally, damn good ballplayers was in any sense demeaning.''

When the Media Says "No"

Far more of a problem for W.R. Grace, though, was a later TV commercial in the same series. It was entitled ''The Deficit Trials: 2017 A.D.'' and dealt with the nation's mounting deficit. Late in 1985, the three television networks unanimously rejected this commercial. That same year the nation's debt reached $2 trillion. As of this writing, incidentally, the debt has soared to more than $3 trillion.

Only a year before, ABC and NBC had accepted another W.R. Grace commercial on the same issue, offering the same underlying proposition, namely, that deficit growth was an issue of increasing significance for all citizens to consider. In rejecting the new commercial, all three networks argued that it dealt with ''a controversial issue of public importance.'' They contended that if the commercial were aired, the Fairness Doctrine would entitle those with dissenting points of view to petition the networks for equal and free commercial time.

W. R. Grace contended that the Fairness Doctrine was not applicable, that merely raising the issue of large deficits was not in and of itself controversial. *Solutions,* they agreed, were controversial, but they were posing no solutions. Was there anything controversial in suggesting that unchecked deficit growth could be unhealthy for future generations?

First Amendment Implications

Grace believed strongly that the refusal of the networks implied more than a mere rejection of a single commercial. They felt this rejection held implications bordering on First Amendment rights, and so they decided to bring the matter before the public.

In so doing Grace had these three basic objectives:

1. To enlist the support of the press and the public for the initiation of constructive negotiations at the networks.

Courtesy of W. R. Grace & Co.

2. To broaden public awareness of the dangers of unchecked deficit growth while gaining positive visibility for the company.

3. To clarify and perhaps liberalize network guidelines for the acceptability of issue advertising.

A Combined Communications Effort

The approach was three-pronged, consisting of

1. A nationwide press relations program, using print, radio, and TV.

2. An advertising effort featuring the airing of the controversial commercial on local, cable, and syndicated television, as well as a print ad on "Trials."

3. Legal assistance targeted initially at the three networks.

Interest by the press in the debate was quickly evident. Every wire service covered the controversy. Editorials appeared in the *Wall Street Journal,* the *New York Times,* and *USA Today.* Magazine coverage included *Time, People, New York Magazine,* and all major media trade books.

All three networks carried pieces on the debate, as did CNN, FNN, and many syndicated programs. Op-ed pieces were prepared for the newspapers, and Chairman Peter Grace delivered 48 speeches and follow-up interviews.

Unable to use the networks, W.R. Grace used close to a million dollars to air the commercial nationwide for five months on cable, local, and syndicated programming, on two Washington network affiliates and in Washington movie theaters. The print ad produced 1,176 responses.

During this time, legal counsel was contacting the three networks with an in-depth written appeal, while sounding out attitudes privately with influentials in the Congress and at the FCC.

That W.R. Grace made its point to the public as well as to the press is clearly evidenced by the thousands of letters of support the company received.

In the end, CBS approved the commercial and established a revised network guideline that would enable advertisers to air issue commercials. ABC reviewed its guidelines, too, while NBC maintained that its own were not restrictive.

On the whole it was a victory, but unfortunately of the Pyrrhic variety. The cost of the effort, including legal fees, had used up W.R. Grace's budget for additional corporate advertising. That particular campaign, having done much to keep the American public informed on some rather pressing issues, and having contributed much to a broader and more positive public image for Grace, had come to its end. At least for a while.

Mobil Corporation:
"Why Do We Buy This Space?"

Perhaps of all the many users of corporate advocacy advertising, Mobil Oil presents the most familiar face to the general public. For many years they have run weekly op-ed ads on a broad spectrum of subjects.

Initially these ads were conceived to counteract some of the publicly held misconceptions of the energy crisis of the 1970s. With so much anti–oil company sentiment carried at that time by the press, Mobil felt that they deserved a chance to present their side of the case. With this in view, they started what became a classic advertising campaign.

Mobil's reasons behind the campaign were perhaps best established in one of the ads appearing in 1981 and carrying the headline: "Why do we buy this space?" Opening copy reads: "For more than 12 years now, we've been addressing Americans with weekly messages in the principal print media. We've argued, cajoled, thundered, pleaded, reasoned and poked fun. In return, we've been reviled, revered, held up as a model, and put down as a sorry example.

"Why does Mobil choose to expose itself to these weekly judgments in the court of public opinion? . . . Our answer is that business needs voices in the media, the same way labor unions, consumers, and other groups in our society do. Our nation functions best when economic and other concerns of the people are subjected to rigorous debate. When our messages add to the spectrum of facts and opinion available to the public, even if the decisions are contrary to our preferences, then the effort and cost are worthwhile."

The ad winds up: "We still continue to speak on a wide array of topics, even though there's no immediate energy crisis to kick around anymore. Because we don't want to be like the mother-in-law who comes to visit only when she has problems and matters to complain about. We think a continuous presence in this space makes sense for us. And we hope, on your part, you find us informative occasionally, or entertaining, or at least infuriating. But never boring. After all, you did read this far, didn't you?"

THREE MAJOR ISSUES WITH ONE CAMPAIGN

Herb Schmertz, formerly Mobil Oil's vice president for public affairs, is a well-known and uniquely successful exponent of issue advertising. The creator of Mobil's landmark op-ed series, he recounts its story in his book, *Good-bye to the Low Profile.* He writes:

In 1970, when our op-ed program began in the *New York Times,* there were at least three major issues facing the oil industry. First, we at Mobil were concerned that in the relatively near future, America and the rest of the free world would be vulnerable to politically motivated oil cutoffs from foreign governments. . . . The United States was becoming increasingly reliant on foreign sources of energy . . . [and] this was bound to have significant and possibly even dangerous effects on the political, social, and economic fabric of our nation.

. . . the environment was our second major concern. . . . Everybody was in favor of clean air and clean water . . . but we were the ones who had to worry about the cost of these programs. . . . It was clear to us that there would have to be some trade-offs between what was ideal and what was realistic.

The third issue that concerned us was that American business institutions were under fire as never before. . . . the oil industry in particular had suffered a significant erosion in public confidence. . . . We knew we had to make a significant response.[4]

KEEPING AN EYE ON THE BASICS

In putting their campaign together, Mobil paid special attention to the basics. They were aware that the *New York Times* had recently instituted what soon became known as the op-ed page—another editorial page opposite the original one. Image would be the only form of advertising allowed on the page. It was a great new media concept and opportunity, and Mobil was quick to seize it, signing up for 13 insertions.

Having committed themselves to a media buy, Mobil needed to make some key decisions as to the format and content of the new ads. One thing seemed clear. Because this advertising would deal with vital public issues requiring the utmost in timeliness, Mobil felt they could prepare them faster in-house.

Accuracy was equally important. Because of the campaign's controversial aspects, complete credibility was essential. One simple mistake could jeopardize the entire effort and send hundreds of thousands of dollars down the drain. Even worse, it might destroy public confidence and valuable corporate image. Facts would have to be carefully checked, and the research would be as important as the writing.

As to the copy for those ads, Schmertz says: "When it came to matters of tone and style, we wanted to take the offensive without being offensive. Our messages

---

[4]*Goodbye to the Low Profile,* Herb Schmertz with William Novak, Little, Brown and Company, 1986.

would be urbane and, when possible, good-humored; they would not be pompous or bland. They would comment on issues, but they would also show other facets of our corporate personality by celebrating good works and excoriating ineptitude. Our ads would also, on occasion, serve to wheedle, cajole, josh, and admonish our readers." As to the ads' format, Schmertz insisted on all-type to blend with the *Times*.

Mobil understood from the beginning that the project entailed certain risks. Speaking out would only goad the politicians and other activist groups who opposed the oil industry, and they would welcome the excuse to attack one of its major members. But the risks were worth the potential rewards of informing the general public of the truth.

The corporation also knew that it might take months before any real results were noted. It would be necessary to commit themselves to the long haul. But the general consensus was that without continuity the campaign would not be worth doing.

Research, Creativity, Continuity

Let the reader note that, just as for many of the image advertisers we have already examined, the key words for Mobil were *research, creative,* and *continuity*. In one way or another these three ingredients belong in just about every successful image program: *research* to assure that accurate information of all kinds is funneled into the program; *creativity* to attract and hold readers; *continuity* to give the message life and impact.

TAKING A POSITION AT ODDS WITH CORPORATE INTERESTS

The opening ad in the Mobil op-ed campaign (see illustration) appeared in October 1970 and carried the attention-grabbing headline: "America has the world's best highways and the world's worst mass transit. We hope this ad moves people."

Despite Mobil's inherent stake in the use of automobiles, they understood that the United States urgently needed more and better mass transit. This was especially true in view of the possibility of an oil shortage.

This first ad generated quite a stir. Writes Schmertz:

> Many readers paid attention simply because the position we took seemed to be at odds with our basic economic interest. Certainly this was the first time that a major oil company had come out publicly for improved public transportation. By questioning the wisdom of continuing to build expensive

America has the world's best highways And the world's worst mass transit.

We hope this ad moves people...

In recent years the United States has developed a really superb highway system. It's been built with tax revenues earmarked specifically for road building.

But the highway construction boom has been accompanied by a mass transit bust. Train and bus travel in this country, with few exceptions, is decrepit. The air traveler suffers increasing indignities despite bigger, faster planes.

Greater New York is a typical example. You can depend on commuting to and from Manhattan—but only to be undependable and slow. On public transport, the 25 miles to Westfield, N.J. takes 75 minutes at an average speed of 20 miles per hour. The 33 miles to Stamford, Conn. takes 60 minutes at 33 mph. The 26 miles to Hicksville, L.I. takes 55 minutes at 28 mph. When you're on time.

You have to be a stoic with stamina to use public ground transportation for a trip beyond the commuting range. Fly to a nearby city? You can hardly get at our congested air terminals, either by land or air. The ride to or from the airport often takes longer than the flight.

Mass transit seems to work better abroad. Americans are agreeably impressed by the fast, comfortable, and attractive subways in foreign cities. Intercity trains in other countries make ours look pitiful. Japan's high-speed Tokaido line carries more than 200,000 passengers a day. Clean, comfortable French, German, Italian, and British trains regularly attain speeds over 100 mph. European railroads are already planning or building expresses that will do better than 150 mph.

Yet, in the United States, new mass transit systems are for the most part still in the wild blue yonder.

Providing for our future transportation needs will require very large expenditures. We believe there's an urgent need for legislators to reexamine the procedures used to generate and expend transportation revenues. Such a review may yield the conclusion that special earmarked funds are no longer the best approach.

In weighing priorities, no decision-maker can ignore the increasing congestion on those fine highways of ours, especially in and around the great urban centers. But more and better mass transit could stop traffic jams before they start. Just one rail line has triple the people-moving capacity of a three-lane superhighway.

It costs less—in energy consumption and in money—to move people via mass transit than on highways. Thus mass transit means less air pollution.

It also means conservation. Whether the energy comes from gasoline for cars, or fuel oil, natural gas, or coal for electric power plants, it's derived from a diminishing natural resource. So we think all forms of transportation should be brought into a national plan for safe, rapid, economical ways of moving people—consistent with the wisest use of our energy resources.

While Mobil sells fuels and lubricants, we don't believe the gasoline consumed by a car idling in a traffic jam (carrying a single passenger, probably) is the best possible use of America's limited petroleum resources. Our products ought to help more people get where they want to go.

To us, that means a green light for mass transit . . . soon.

Courtesy of Mobil Corporation.

highways, we infuriated several constituencies that had traditionally been our allies, including the heavy-equipment industry, the construction industry, and, most of all, the other major oil companies. These groups saw our advocacy of mass transit as a betrayal, and they didn't hesitate to let us know of their disappointment.

By the time the initial 13-ad schedule was completed, it was apparent to Mobil that their messages had not only been noticed and read, but also discussed and reprinted. The series continued sporadically at that point until the decision was made to go to a weekly schedule.

That Mobil is more than satisfied with the results should be clear, considering that (as of this writing) the ads, as feisty as ever, still run every week.

As we mentioned at the beginning of this chapter, much advocacy advertising is highly controversial. Mobil's certainly fits this description. It tends to provoke extreme reactions, both pro and con. Many praise Mobil's stand for "recognizing opposing views and presenting corporate positions in a positive way; others accuse it of being too strident and preaching to the converted."[5]

When you're selling ideas instead of products—as in image advertising—it is difficult to quantify results. But Mobil is convinced that their advocacy program has brought some challenging points of view to the attention of the public. Research agrees. Apparently, at least some of the company's key publics now understand that the oil industry is "neither monolithic nor antediluvian."

A final word from Schmertz: "Over the years, we've also had a lot to say about the role of business in American life. On a number of occasions we've used our space to explain and defend America's economic system, which has been so little understood by our own citizens. We have supported efforts to reduce the federal deficit, and we've paid particular attention to private-sector reports on how the federal government can cut spending. Finally, we have been outspoken about the media's negative treatment of big business."

How Do You Choose Your Issue?

To make any issue work effectively for your company, choose it carefully and be sure you can bring important new information or a new perspective to the discussion. Remember, you may not be able to change public opinion, but you

---

[5]"Corporate Advertising: Stacking the Odds," *Grey Matter,* Grey Advertising Inc., 1983, Vol. 54, Number 2.

Earth, rising

Late on any Friday afternoon, in any business, you'll see people heading out for the hills. And the beaches. And the ski slopes. Wherever. Then they trundle in—at times are trundled in—on Monday morning, back from the great outdoors and ready for another tussle with the profit plan. Can anyone sincerely believe that these are foes of the environment?

This is not to say that industry's record on cherishing the natural environment is unblemished. Whose record is? What was thought customary and even harmless decades ago—such as hiking across a pristine alpine meadow—is now frowned upon because the marks of passage remain visible for years afterwards. There are oil refineries built once upon a time in the middle of nowhere that are surrounded today by thriving communities. What was harmless in the middle of nowhere seems not so harmless in the middle of town. Times change—but business has changed, too. We think we're just as friendly with the earth as are our critics.

That's why confrontation, as if there were no reasonable path between two camps labeled business and environmentalism, is so wasteful. We don't see two camps. Energies that ought to be joined in collaborative efforts are far less productively employed when slinging gibes or lawsuits. When we work in tandem—or at least pull in the same direction—a lot gets done.

● In Florida, where Mobil has mined over the past 15 years phosphate rock from about 9200 acres, the reclamation process goes hand in hand with our mining plan. More than 2800 of the mined acres have already been restored. Farmers now graze cattle on grassy pastureland that once was a mine.

● At our Caballo Rojo coal mine in Wyoming, even the fencing was specially designed, after consultation with wildlife biologists, to let pronghorn antelope move across and around our land as easily as mule deer.

● We keep 650 professionals working full-time on environmental, health, and safety programs, and last year alone spent about $780 million on programs to protect and improve the environment. And Mobil is just one company among thousands.

● Though we already recycle all our plastic scrap and buy another 100 million pounds from others for recycling in our manufacturing processes, Mobil Chemical also has a national program with interested supermarkets to recycle plastic grocery sacks. We are a founder with seven other companies of the National Polystyrene Recycling Co. And its goal is to recycle at least 25 percent of all food-service and packaging polystyrene by 1995.

This same sort of active environmentalism now imbues businesses and industries all across the land. A major chemical company voluntarily suspended production of a compound said to cause pollution—a product whose annual sales volume amounted to $750 million. Another company putting up a power plant in New England allotted $2 million for planting trees in Central America to offset the new plant's emission of carbon dioxide. The auto and oil industries have joined forces to identify a vehicle-fuels system that will further reduce auto emissions. And so it goes.

An old saying in business is that people have to look at the big picture. And the big picture today is that famous one of earth rising, taken from the moon. Business has seen it too. We get the picture.

Mobil®

Where's the rip-off?

The sharp increase in gasoline prices has sparked thousands of words, most of them accusing the oil industry of reaping undeserved profits. Industry spokesmen have attempted to respond, with little apparent success.

So we decided to let the numbers do the talking.

West Texas Intermediate is a benchmark domestic crude oil. We've translated the price per barrel on the spot market to cents per gallon, and tracked the price movement from early July to last Tuesday. Gasoline also trades on the spot market, and we've shown the average spot price of regular unleaded across the U.S.

Finally, we've shown the average price we charged our dealers in 29 key cities for regular unleaded, along with the price for Mobil distributors. The dealers account for 70 percent and the distributors for about 30 percent of our gasoline business.

	CRUDE/PRODUCT PRICES JULY 3, AUGUST 7					
(All numbers cents/gallon)	7/3/90	7/17/90	*7/31/90	**8/2/90	8/7/90	Increase 7/3–8/7
West Texas Intermediate Spot Market Crude	40.2	44.4	48.1	55.5	70.5	+ 30.3
†Regular Unleaded Spot Market Gasoline	60.4	63.7	62.8	68.9	85.1	+ 24.7
Average Mobil Price to Dealer Regular Unleaded	74.5	73.6	74.7	75.0	81.2	+ 6.7
Average Mobil Price to Distributor Regular Unleaded	67.8	68.0	69.6	69.8	78.3	+ 10.5

* OPEC Met July 26 – 27
**Iraq Invaded Kuwait August 2
†Platt's Low Weighted Average

The table shows that market prices for both crude oil and gasoline rose far more sharply than Mobil's.

One final observation: Much crude is now bought on terms specifying that the price is to be set by the spot market at the time of delivery. So the price of the gasoline you buy today was not set in concrete weeks ago.

Mobil®

Courtesy of Mobil Corporation.

want at least to have your viewpoint heard by the people who can be influential in your cause.

Whether anyone pays attention depends on the quality of the ideas you present, and the way in which you present them. In other words, what you say will be only as effective as how you say it. But whether the public agrees with you or not, people generally will respect a company that goes out on a limb for its beliefs.

Like W.R. Grace, pick an issue for which your company may be perceived as having enlightened self-interest as well as concern for the community and nation. Grace started with a campaign opposing an increase in the capital gains tax, and then moved on to such national issues as productivity and the deficit.

United Technologies Corporation concentrated on the relationship between individual performance and national performance. Mobil Oil first concentrated on the prospect of an energy shortage; this was followed by ads on environmental problems, the erosion of public confidence in business, and other economic and political issues.

All of the these are tremendous subjects for advocacy advertising, but there are plenty of other vital issues of national or community significance to choose from. Select the one—or ones—best suited to your company's involvements and projected image. Then do the necessary research to help you decide what stand your company should take. Design a communications program that will present your position dramatically, credibly, and convincingly. And finally, back up your program with the necessary financing to keep it running in the appropriate media long enough to have the proper effect.

The campaign and the issue it espouses may have little or nothing to do with how a corporation conducts its business, but the attention that the company—and its CEO—receives can have a major positive effect on corporate image.

CHAPTER SEVEN

Managing a Crisis:
Frontline Defense
When the World Falls Apart

"Cyanide in a popular analgesic . . ."

"Glass in the leading baby food . . ."

"A major oil spill . . ."

"Poison gas leaking into a sleeping city . . ."

"Benzene in natural sparkling mineral water . . ."

The problem with emergencies is that you seldom really know when one is going to strike. Just ask Johnson & Johnson, Union Carbide, Gerber, Exxon, Perrier, and a host of other blue chip corporations. They weren't looking for trouble, but they found it—or, more precisely, it found them—and generally with tragic results.

Sometimes the crisis doesn't even exist. It's just an unfounded rumor. Procter & Gamble knows that. So do Xerox, Life Savers, and many more.

An Investment in the Future

The possibility of disaster striking at any time is one very good reason to be sure your corporation has a well-defined, positive corporate image. It's a sound investment, an insurance policy against the unpredictability of the future. Anyone who doubts the long-term value of corporate image need only study the Johnson & Johnson Tylenol tragedy.

The Tylenol story is a familiar one. It's been told and retold and need not be especially detailed here. Suffice it to say that when, in September 1982, five deaths all pointed to the sabotage of bottles of Tylenol, Johnson & Johnson and their McNeil Consumer Products subsidiary had their work cut out.

Only because of a well-established, positive image of concern for social responsibility, a long history of careful management, and household-friendly, quality products was Johnson & Johnson able to prevent permanent damage to the company and its reputation. In other words, the company's excellent public image had created a "reservoir of good will"[1] which now helped them to weather an extremely dangerous storm.

Fast, Bold Action

This takes nothing away from the speedy, intelligent response Johnson & Johnson gave to the crisis. The immediate move to recall all Tylenol capsules from the marketplace and withdraw Tylenol product advertising, and the decision to answer any and all press inquiries started the process of putting the top-selling analgesic back on track.

Two months later Johnson & Johnson announced the reintroduction of Tylenol with innovative new tamper-proof packaging and coupons to enable customers to replace any old packages they might still have. By January Tylenol ads were running again. In little more than three months Tylenol had regained its momentum and was fast approaching the market share it had enjoyed before the crisis.

---

[1]Reprinted from "Parables for Peers," *Business Week.*

Fast, bold action coupled with a long-standing corporate image of public trust helped Johnson & Johnson bounce back in a relatively short time from a tragedy that might have left permanent scars.

When Reality and Perception Clash

Four years later, in 1986, Johnson & Johnson suffered its second poison scare when a woman died of cyanide ingestion traced to Tylenol capsules. Again, the product was withdrawn, and the company launched extensive advertising announcing both the recall and the decision to stop producing Tylenol in capsules but to make the product in a tamper-proof caplet form instead.

That same year, another company with a similar situation took a different course. Gerber Products Company, the largest U.S. baby food producer, was faced with a wave of complaints that glass had been found in the baby food. Believing that the charges would eventually be proven false, Gerber decided to keep its product on the market and ride out the storm.

They felt that this was not a case of product quality, but rather of public perception—or, actually, misperception. If Gerber was wrong in this belief, results could be disastrous.

Discrepancies between Gerber and Tylenol Cases

There were important differences, however, between the glass scare and the capsule poisoning. For one thing, people died from the poisoned capsules. The most serious of the unsubstantiated claims against the baby food was a cut lip.

Then, too, the Tylenol problem had been localized: five deaths in Chicago in 1982 and one in New York in 1986. Baby food complaints occurred in 40 states and in more than half the cases, complainants called the media before notifying local authorities, the FDA, or Gerber. According to James Lovejoy, Gerber's director of corporate communications: "Media myopia ignored the overall picture, and reporters were interested only in the local angle of specific claims on which they often had more information—albeit one-sided—than anyone else."

Tylenol was a single brand, and before the poisonings few consumers knew that Johnson & Johnson was the parent company. On the other hand, the Gerber name was on 168 separate food products and complaints were not isolated to any one or two. Lovejoy says: "To recall one or more products as a public relations ploy to demonstrate concern, without documented proof of the cause or corrective action, clearly would only confuse mothers and would betray our employees who are totally committed to maintaining Gerber's heritage of being unexcelled in quality control.''

The only real connection between the baby food and Tylenol incidents was in the timing. The first report of glass in Gerber baby food—phone calls by a New York woman to New York television stations—came just three days after a New York woman died from poisoned Tylenol. This was enough to create preconceived perceptions in the minds of some reporters, perceptions that precluded objectivity.

With the first complaint Gerber moved quickly. They obtained the jar of peaches alleged to contain glass from the consumer and expressed it to their lab along with samples of like code produced at the same time. New York State health officials also picked up samples for testing.

Unfortunately, before the tests could be completed, a local TV station pressured two chain store outlets to remove Gerber baby food from their shelves. The wire services picked up the story, and by the time New York health officials gave Gerber a clean bill of health, copycat complaints were coming in from all over. There was no pattern to the complaints, either by type of product, retail outlet, warehouse, shipping point, manufacturing site or date of processing. But complaints continued to grow and the media clamored for a recall.

Touch All Communication Bases

Lovejoy continues: ''We adopted a no-recall strategy unless justified by the facts. Based on research showing the FDA enjoys higher credibility than any company . . . we also decided our communications effort should rely heavily on the agency's data and spokespersons to present the truth on baby food safety. While continuing to respond to local press calls that totaled up to 80 per day, we kicked off a pro-active communications effort . . .''

All bases were touched. A continuing program of news releases and updates, plant tours, and interviews with the CEO, Gerber's director of research and quality control, and the FDA commissioner all helped switch the media and wire services from blowing every unconfirmed local complaint into a national event.

Another critical audience, trade customers, was kept as up-to-date as possible, with news releases telefaxed or mailed overnight. And Gerber's 700-person sales force helped their customers by calling on overzealous local media and news directors to convince them no health hazard was involved. Most trade magazines supported Gerber after learning the facts. Communication with employees, investors, government authorities, and health care providers was also important and was handled with equal care and professionalism.

Gerber Baby Roars

Key to the entire program was an aggressive consumer communications effort to stop the erosion that research said was taking place within the customer base. A direct-mail message was sent out to the 2.6 million households that included a baby. That message drew more than 250,000 replies, three-quarters of which were favorable.

While the nightly news was putting Gerber down with undocumented claims, Gerber responded with major television advertising. Commercials invited customers to call or write their questions. Network lawyers held up these ads until they could review the answers, but, says Lovejoy, "the Gerber baby roared at this point and network management overruled the lawyers."

What was the payoff? In a few months Gerber's market share rebounded to about where it had been before the glass scare. The nation's young mothers—always a careful, knowledgeable consumer group—recognized that Gerber had been a victim, not a villain. Gerber's initial instinct that the complaints had no foundation was accepted as correct; they had successfully met the crisis head-on without recalling the product.

Lovejoy adds: "There is no magic formula or 'right way' to handle a crisis. Should you ever be faced with a real or alleged product tampering situation, I guarantee your response will not be dictated by a textbook solution. The variables of your corporate culture, your market, the product involved, the source of the complaint, your company's previous complaint history, and many other factors will give each situation a personality and priority of its own."

When—and Where—You Least Expect It

Gerber was fortunate. Their particular crisis didn't end in death. Tylenol, in two separate incidents, was affected by the senseless deaths of six innocent people. Union Carbide, however, was faced with claims that more than 2,000 people had died, with thousands more maimed for life.

During the night of December 3, 1984, poisonous gas had leaked from a tank of methyl isocyanate at a plant in Bhopal, India, and spread throughout that city of one million while residents slept. The plant was owned and operated by Union Carbide India Limited, which had celebrated its fiftieth anniversary that same year. The company had 14 plants, 5 operating divisions, 9,000 employees, and one of the best safety records of all Indian industrial firms.

The problems raised by this tragedy spanned two companies, two governments, two continents, and two profoundly different cultures. And Union Carbide's image took a beating on both sides of the world.

INITIAL DECISIONS WRITE THE CRISIS SCRIPT

When the first communications about the Bhopal tragedy reached Union Carbide Corporation headquarters in Danbury, Connecticut, at 4:00 A.M. on December 3, there was devastating shock as well as grief. Reliable, firsthand information was difficult to come by as there were only two phone lines out of Bhopal, and they were tenuous even in the best of times.

Despite this lack of hard information, Union Carbide management was able to make several vital decisions in a matter of hours. First, there was a general consensus that the corporation should assume moral responsibility and provide emergency relief for the victims. To underscore this, the company made an offer of $1 million in emergency relief. In addition, Chairman Warren Anderson would accompany a medical/technical team to India. (Shortly after his arrival Anderson was placed under house arrest by the Indian government but was soon released.)

Union Carbide also created a special Bhopal crisis team, allowing the rest of top management to concentrate on running the business. Ronald S. Wishart, vice president for public affairs, was named Anderson's chief of staff and Bhopal team leader. At the same time the important step was taken to make the company accessible to the media and to share whatever information could be obtained.

Comments Wishart: "Actions taken in the first few hours—some say 30 minutes—pretty much write the script for the balance of a crisis. Implicit in that is the belief you'll have the facts. In the case of Bhopal, however, we were receiving much of our information from the press, and it was sketchy at best."[2]

KEEP ALL PUBLICS INFORMED

In the days immediately following the incident, Union Carbide headquarters received as many as 500 calls a day from U.S. and overseas media people, people with relatives in India, people who wanted to help, and scientists and others who wanted information.

The company organized press conferences and press tours, and it made management available for interviews. Special briefings, too, were held for various congressmen and other government officials.

Employees were kept up-to-date on a continuing basis via employee news

---

[2]"Managing Trouble," Ronald S. Wishart, Vice President, Public Affairs, Union Carbide Corporation, Remarks at Blumenthal Conference on Business Ethics, May 2, 1987.

bulletins and company house organs, videotapes, and employee meetings. In like manner stockholders and security analysts were informed throughout as to developments.

With election time near at hand in India, it seemed that every politician was hunting votes by vilifying Union Carbide. In the United States, an ill-conceived story, suggesting a possible shutdown of the corporation, made headlines that put the company's stock price into a steep slide. On the day the story appeared the stock dropped $5.75 to $38.75, and it bottomed out a few days later at $32.75, its lowest price for the year.

Wishart remembers: "We believed we'd need to address problems and publics throughout the U.S., in India and the third world, Britain and Europe, and for that matter, throughout the world. We'd need to make our voice heard in the New York and international financial communities, in Washington, and in state capitals. We needed to teach some of our people how to talk with TV reporters, and to show plant management how to expand and improve communications with their communities."

Accepting Responsibility

The tremendous number of casualties halfway around the world and the difficulty in getting accurate information were not the only reasons Bhopal presented a unique challenge. The incident happened to one company, Union Carbide India Ltd., but responsibility for it, both in the states and in India, was placed to a great degree on the shoulders of another—Union Carbide Corporation.

Keep in mind that Union Carbide India Ltd. was an Indian-run organization, with its own management and board of directors, and a 100 percent Indian work force; and it was subject to Indian laws and regulations. There had been no Americans involved with the company since 1982. Union Carbide Corporation owned about 51 percent of the stock, and the Indian government about 24 percent.

Then, too, evidence indicated that the incident was no accident. Everything pointed to a discontented employee who had connected a hose to the tank and added several hundred gallons of water. The evidence was convincing to all who looked at it, with the exception of the Indian government.

Why then did Union Carbide accept the moral responsibility while denying the legal responsibility? Wishart explains:

There were two reasons. To world opinion, Union Carbide was the company involved. It was our logo on the gate. Turning our backs on the victims under those circumstances would have compounded the damage to our reputation.

Union Carbide is a concerned corporation, and we wanted the world to know it. We didn't want to be the victims' adversary. Beyond that, courts and juries are unpredictable, which is the reason defendants and plaintiffs settle their cases out of court in more than 95 percent of all such cases. They do it even if convinced that the facts and the law are on their side.

The case dragged on in the courts for four years. Initial furor subsided eventually, but Union Carbide maintained efforts to keep all interested publics informed. In 1989 the affair came to its official end when the Supreme Court of India directed an out-of-court settlement for $470 million, to cover all claims arising out of the tragedy, to which both parties agreed.

But even then problems remained to haunt all concerned. Story after story in both U.S. and Indian papers tell of major criticisms of the settlement and even fraud in the matter of compensation for the gas vicitms.

The Best Crisis System Needs Backup of Positive Image

Did Union Carbide handle their corporate communications as well as possible? Says Wishart: "How well you manage communications during a crisis will probably reflect how well you've managed all along. You're off to a fast start if you have the systems in place—and operating."

Union Carbide had no crisis management system in place, but they were quick to organize a crisis team, quick to put it into operation, quick to make some of the right responses. Whatever corporate image they had was seriously threatened, and there was no defense, no reservoir of goodwill. It had been years since the company had run any appreciable image advertising. Many of Union Carbide's constituencies, including the general public, knew little about the corporation, its basic values and policies of social concern.

This, of course, was a fundamental difference between Bhopal and the Tylenol problem. Union Carbide had little if any image. The man on the street didn't know what it was or what it did. It was just some big, faceless American corporation that apparently had killed all these Indians.

Johnson & Johnson was a different situation. They had been around a long time and had a very familiar name. Comments one expert in the image advertising field: "Their products fit right in with diapers and babies—powder and no tears in your eyes. Babies—blue, pink, soft, cuddly! They had that image going for them. They also had a line of medical products going for them . . . products that heal people. Healing people is good; killing people is bad. Johnson & Johnson heals people and cares for babies. That's their image and it's been in people's minds for a half a century.''

The people were willing to trust Johnson & Johnson. The company could position itself as a victim. Their product, Tylenol, had been poisoned by some outside, bad person. J&J had only to demonstrate that they were intent on protecting their product as best they could from further outside tampering.

Union Carbide, on the other hand, appeared to have a product that had misfunctioned in some way; the error was on the company's part. The fundamental willingness to believe in the corporation was just not there as it was for Johnson & Johnson.

Not every company has a product that becomes a reliable, recognizable part of the public's everyday life. Those that don't must work harder to earn the public's trust and friendship. This takes time, years of trust-building activities with employees, communities, shareholders, the media, and all the other publics—and the consistent use of convincing image advertising.

Six Key Steps to Crisis Management

No matter how good your image advertising or how well you've built the trust of your publics, you can't always prevent a crisis. Careful planning may take the edge off, but you still have to face it, manage it, survive it.

Different companies approach crisis in different ways. There obviously can be no set ''right'' way. Just as every company is different, so is every crisis. Each has its own guidelines and needs its own kind of attention. But one rule holds true no matter the company, no matter the crisis: the better prepared the corporation may be, the better its chances of surviving the blow.

Here are six simple steps to follow to help your company maintain control of its own destiny when disaster strikes and the world seems to fall apart.

1. *Be prepared. Have a plan of action.*　We are in an era of corporate crisis planning. Few major companies today would consider not having some kind of action plan should an emergency arise.

Jack O'Brien is the former president of McNeil Pharmaceutical, Spring House, Pennsylvania, a Johnson & Johnson company. Now retired, O'Brien headed McNeil during the Tylenol troubles, and he has this to say about crisis management: ''When a crisis develops, corporations don't have time to work out these details. Being prepared and involved with your target audiences and the media invariably results in a faster recovery of your credibility—and ultimately your corporate image.''[3]

Some corporations print up detailed emergency manuals, which outline what should be done, who should do it, and who should be contacted in the event of unexpected problems. Another technique is to put your company through periodic simulations of emergency situations. No warning is generally given, although employees should be advised that it is only a drill.

2. *Build a crisis management team.* A trained team of key executives and technicians, representing the fundamental diciplines of the corporation, should be on call at all times. These are people who will know what to do. They will know how to remedy a given situation, and how to deal with and mollify hostile media and other groups.

The company without a crisis team should at least have a trained spokesperson on staff—someone with the title and authority to represent the company in any given situation. He or she might even rehearse answers to tough anticipated questions projected for various possible crisis scenarios.

Crises, of course, are not limited to corporations. In September 1988, a young man, armed with a semi-automatic rifle, took 11 hostages in an Armed Forces Recruiting Station in suburban Richmond, Virginia. Three of the hostages were U.S. Navy petty officers.

A Navy crisis reaction team swung into action. The team included not only public affairs officers but a licensed social worker from a nearby Navy Family Services Center to help ease the burden on the families of the hostages. The team was well trained and rehearsed to deal effectively with members of its own ''corporate'' family, as well as the media and local authorities.

3. *Respond quickly but not hastily.* Says Mike Todd, Lieutenant Commander, U.S. Navy, and an experienced public affairs officer: ''Prepare for a crisis *before* it happens. . . . Prepare a crisis communications plan that can be put into place *quickly*. Make sure that several people are aware of the plan, so everything does not hinge on one person who might not be reachable in an emergency.''[4]

Johnson & Johnson was prepared to move immediately to withdraw Tylenol

---

[3]''Corporations Improve Crisis Communications Plans,'' Tom Eisenhart, *Business Marketing,* July 1990.

[4]''Helping Internal Audiences Cope,'' Mike Todd, Lieutenant Commander U.S. Navy, *Public Relations Journal,* June 1989.

from the marketplace and cancel its advertising. This decisive action helped convince the public of Johnson & Johnson's social conscience and concern. Gerber also made an important decision at the start—to keep their product *on* the market. They put little credence in the glass scare and didn't wish to further upset consumers with unnecessary recalls.

4. *Work cooperatively with the media.* You need the media on your side—or at least neutral. You may need all the support you can get, and the media can help you get it. They are vital to telling your story to government, financial, consumer, and other influential groups.

Johnson & Johnson knew this and quickly made the decision to answer all questions from the media and cooperate with them fully. Gerber knew, too, and decided on a proactive communications effort with the media and all of their target publics.

5. *Don't panic!* No crisis game plan could have foreseen the terrible magnitude of Union Carbide's particular emergency. Nor was there a crisis team in place. That the company was able to respond so quickly and so effectively— especially with little information to go on—is a credit to an experienced management's clearheaded thinking. They were able to assess the situation and make the right moves without letting potential disaster panic them down blind alleys.

6. *Take out image insurance.* In this day and age, when almost anything is possible if not probable, it seems only good corporate sense to be prepared for the unpredictable worst. Union Carbide wasn't prepared. It didn't have the same kind of established image to fall back upon as did Johnson & Johnson and Gerber. Consequently they took more public criticism on almost all levels than perhaps was necessary. The front-page stories of a possible company shutdown did a lot of damage at the time and although the company was insured and solvent, the stories still haunt the memories of Union Carbide executives.

From *The Wall Street Journal on Marketing:* "In the mid-1960s, Union Carbide was a corporate image advertiser. When chemical companies were under attack for producing material for use in the Vietnam War, Union Carbide didn't drop in opinion polls conducted by Opinion Research Corporation. Du Pont and Dow Chemical Co., however, didn't advertise and lost favor with the public. And when Union Carbide later reduced its ad spending, favorable attitudes toward the company also declined, according to the Opinion Research study."[5]

There are probably as many ways to prepare for and handle a crisis as there are potential crises. Choose the system that best suits your company's needs and philosophy. The important thing to remember is that whatever happens you'll find it a good deal easier to deal with your emergency if your corporation is insured by a solid, positive image.

In other words, you need corporate image advertising especially when times are good and all is going well, in order to protect your image when things get hot.

---

[5] *The Wall Street Journal on Marketing,* Ronald Alsop, Bill Abrams: Dow Jones-Irwin and Co., Homewood, IL, 1986.

CHAPTER EIGHT

Retaining Quality Employees:
Using Image to Recruit and Keep the Best

■ Preceding chapters have gone into they whys and wherefores of six key reasons for image advertising:[1]

1. Building awareness and acceptance.

2. Redefining a corporation after some major change.

3. Helping pre-sell a product.

4. Impacting shareholders and the financial world.

5. Presenting a company's position on key issues.

6. Crisis management.

---

[1]"Why Corporate Advertising?" A marketing report from *Time* magazine, 1983.

This chapter covers the seventh major mission, but this is a mission with a slight difference. The target audience—employees—is a mission in itself, but rarely would image advertising be planned to reach *only* employees. There must be at least one other target audience, which means a need for at least one other kind of mission involved. Such combined programs are sometimes called hybrid campaigns.

Conversely, the image program of almost any corporation almost always includes the company's own employees as at least a secondary public. In some instances—perhaps especially in crisis management—there are those who believe the employee group should always be the *primary* audience.

Glen Broom, a professor of journalism at San Diego State University, has said that "employees should be the first audience addressed because many of them talk to customers. They also talk to neighbors and friends . . . you don't want employees to read about [a crisis] in the papers."[2]

That's why it's important to include an image mission aimed directly at the employee, a program designed to keep the employee knowledgeable and enthusiastic about his or her company. By building a strong company image for your employees, you can look to encourage employee goodwill and loyalty which in turn can attract new workers and foster a cooperative environment in your communities.

Tell Your Employees—
They'll Tell Their Communities

Employees need to know company goals; they need to feel involved in corporate plans. The more communication they receive about the company, the more they will feel a part of the team, a part of the solution. Informed workers can project a positive image for your company within their own communities. One can hardly expect outsiders to accept as truth what company employees do not understand or believe themselves.

Thus good employee relations usually go hand in hand with good community relations.

People like to talk about their jobs and places of work with friends and neighbors; it's human nature. Your employees are no different, and they have the choice of tearing your corporate image down or spreading a good and supportive word.

---

[2]"Corporations Improve Crisis Plans," Tom Eisenhart, *Business Marketing*, July 1990.

High morale among employees will be viewed by the public as a sign that the company strives for quality in its management and organization as well as in its products and services. Employees who reflect either internal satisfaction or conflict can either improve or destroy corporate image and community relations.

You want, of course, the cooperation of your communities. A positive relationship with local media, authorities, and consumers can smooth over a variety of potentially rough situations.

Just as the community has a stake in the success of your business, so does the company have a stake in the health and prosperity of its community. This can become a rather involved relationship. The image of business is far more complex today than it was 20 years ago; now it includes social, welfare, environmental, and political concerns as well as economic.

Consistent image advertising, backed by employee goodwill, does much to achieve the desired relationship by informing the community about company products and services, company policies and goals, and company concerns and awareness.

Consider International Paper's "Power of the Printed Word" series. Highly regarded by employees as well as others, it had "tremendous impact in plant and mill communities"[3] by supporting the success of company products while projecting an image of public service and concern.

An Organization's Primary Target

James Gray, in his recent book, *Managing the Corporate Image,* corroborates the beneficial effect of employee well-being on community relations: "Employees are an organization's primary public, and they should be both respected and treated with fairness. To expect a positive public image when employees complain throughout the immediate community and beyond is unrealistic. But employees whose concerns are taken into account and who are consulted about company policies and goals generally broadcast job satisfaction into the community at large."[4]

Your company's corporate image should be articulated accurately and consistently to your employees and reinforced in every communication to them. Image advertising is in itself an excellent form of employee communication, and is a

---

[3]"Never Underestimate the Power of the Printed Word," speech by Robert F. Lauterborn, January 1988.

[4]*Managing the Corporate Image,* James Gray, Quorum Books, 1986.

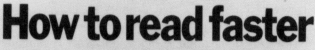

How to read faster

By Bill Cosby

International Paper asked Bill Cosby—who earned his doctorate in education and has been involved in projects which help people learn to read faster—to share what he's learned about reading more in less time.

When I was a kid in Philadelphia, I must have read every comic book ever published. (There were fewer of them then than there are now.)

I zipped through all of them in a couple of days, then reread the good ones until the next issues arrived.

Yes indeed, when I was a kid, the reading game was a snap.

But as I got older, my eyeballs must have slowed down or something! I mean, comic books started to pile up faster than my brother Russell and I could read them!

It wasn't until much later, when I was getting my doctorate, I realized it wasn't my eyeballs that were to blame. Thank goodness. They're still moving as well as ever.

The problem is, there's too much to read these days, and too little time to read every word of it.

Now, mind you, I still read comic books. In addition to contracts, novels, and newspapers. Screenplays, tax returns and correspondence. Even textbooks about how people read. And which techniques help people read more in less time.

I'll let you in on a little secret. There are hundreds of techniques you could learn to help you read faster. But I know of 3 that are especially good.

And if I can learn them, so can you—and you can put them to use *immediately.*

They are commonsense, practical ways to get the meaning from printed words quickly and efficiently. So you'll have time to enjoy your comic books, have a good laugh with Mark Twain or a good cry with *War and Peace.* Ready?

Okay. The first two ways can help you get through tons of reading material—fast—*without reading every word.*

They'll give you the *overall* meaning of what you're reading. And let you cut out an awful lot of *unnecessary* reading.

1. Preview—if it's long and hard

Previewing is especially useful for getting a general idea of heavy reading like long magazine or newspaper articles, business reports, and nonfiction books.

It can give you as much as half the comprehension in as little as one tenth the time. For example, you should be able to preview eight or ten 100-page reports in an hour. After previewing, you'll be able to decide which reports (or which parts of which reports) are worth a closer look.

Here's how to preview: Read the entire first two paragraphs of whatever you've chosen. Next read only the *first sentence of* each successive paragraph.

"Learn to read faster and you'll have time for a good laugh with Mark Twain—and a good cry with War and Peace.

Then read the entire last two paragraphs.

Previewing doesn't give you all the details. But it does keep you from spending time on things you don't really want—or need—to read. Notice that previewing gives you a quick, overall view of long, *unfamiliar* material. For short, light reading, there's a better technique.

2. Skim—if it's short and simple

Skimming is a good way to get a general idea of light reading—like popular magazines or the sports and entertainment sections of the paper.

You should be able to skim a weekly popular magazine or the second section of your daily paper in less than *half* the time it takes you to read it now.

Skimming is also a great way to review material you've read before.

Here's how to skim: Think of your eyes as magnets. Force them to move fast. Sweep them across each and every line of type. Pick up *only a few key words in each line.*

Everybody skims differently. You and I may not pick up exactly the same words when we skim the same piece, but we'll both get a pretty similar idea of what it's all about.

To show you how it works, I circled the words I picked out when I skimmed the following story. Try it. It shouldn't take you more than 10 seconds.

My brother Russell thinks monsters live in our bedroom closet at night. But I told him he is crazy. "Go and check then," he said. I didn't want to. Russell said I was chicken.

"Am not," I said.
"Are so," he said.
So I told him the monsters were going to eat him at midnight. He started to cry. My Dad came in and told the monsters to beat it. Then he told us to go to sleep.
"If I hear any more about monsters," he said, "I'll spank you." We went to sleep fast. And you know something? They never did come back.

Skimming can give you a very good idea of this story in about half

"Read with a good light—and with as few friends as possible to help you out. No TV, no music. It'll help you concentrate better—and read faster."

the words—and in *less* than half the time it'd take to read every word.
So far, you've seen that previewing and skimming can give you a *general* idea about content—fast. But neither technique can promise more than 50 percent comprehension, because you aren't reading all the words. (Nobody gets something for nothing in the reading game.)
To *read faster and understand must*—if not all—of what you read, you need to know a third technique.

3. Cluster—to increase speed *and* comprehension

Most of us learned to read by looking at each word in a sentence—*one at a time*.
Like this:
My—brother—Russell—thinks—monsters...
You probably still read this way sometimes, especially when the words are difficult. Or when the words have an extra-special meaning—as in a poem, a Shakespearean

play, or a contract. And that's O.K.
But word-by-word reading is a rotten way to read faster. It actually *cuts down* on your speed.
Clustering trains you to look at *groups* of words instead of one at a time—to increase your speed enormously. For most of us, clustering is a *totally different way of seeing what we read.*
Here's how to cluster: Train your eyes to see *all* the words in clusters of up to 3 or 4 words at a glance.
Here's how I'd cluster the story we just skimmed:

My brother Russell thinks monsters live in our bedroom closet at night. But I told him he is crazy.
"Go and check then," he said. I didn't want to Russell said I was chicken.
"Am not," I said.
"Are so," he said.
So I told him the monsters were going to eat him at midnight. He started to cry. My Dad came in and told the monsters to beat it. Then he told us to go to sleep.
"If I hear any more about monsters," he said, "I'll spank you." We went to sleep fast. And you know something? They never did come back.

Learning to read clusters is not something your eyes do naturally. It takes constant practice.
Here's how to go about it: Pick something light to read. Read it as fast as you can. Concentrate on seeing 3 to 4 words at once rather than one word at a time. Then reread

"Preview, skim, and cluster to read faster—except the things you want to read word for word."

the piece at your normal speed to see what you missed the first time.
Try a second piece. First cluster, then reread to see what you missed in this one.
When you can read in clusters without missing much the first time, your speed has increased. Practice 15 minutes every day and you might pick up the technique in a week or so. (But don't be disappointed if it takes longer. Clustering *everything* takes time and practice.)
So now you have 3 ways to help you read faster. Preview to cut down on unnecessary heavy reading. Skim to get a quick, general idea of light reading. And cluster to increase your speed *and* comprehension.
With enough practice, you'll be able to handle *more* reading at school or work—and at home—*in less time*. You should even have enough time to read your favorite comic books—and *War and Peace*!

Bill Cosby

planned factor in many employee relations programs. It can encourage your people to feel good about the place where they work and be happy that friends, neighbors, and relatives recognize the importance, strength, and worth of their company.

The Reader's Digest Association is well aware of this. The goodwill of their employees—and what they know about *Reader's Digest* and what they think about it—is critical to the ultimate success of the company and its related products. This is reflected in the Reader's Digest corporate mission statement, "Our Corporate Values: Words We Live By," where close to the top of the list we find the section "Recognition and Concern for Employees."

THE TIP OF THE ICEBERG

The current Reader's Digest image advertising is aimed at telling business and advertising executives some facts they may not know about the company. Equally important, the campaign is also intended to inform employees and make them feel proud to be part of the Reader's Digest family.

Everyone knows *Reader's Digest,* the magazine, but not everyone knows Reader's Digest, the corporation—that their books are guaranteed best-sellers and that their music packages sell in the millions and that they offer home videos. Many people are surprised to learn of the magnitude of the company as a global publisher and one of the world's leading direct mail marketers.

Equally pertinent, management wants its employees to know all their products—not just their own particular corner of the business. The company wants employees to understand the basis of the Reader's Digest product line and why it is expert at what it does, and wants them to be able to articulate the concept and have a sense of pride in the company.

Typical ads in this series of four-color pages—"Banner business" and "Local accents" (see illustrations)—explain that the magazine "is the consummate international publication . . . and that's only part of what we do." Some of the other ads have highlighted Condensed Books, General Books, Music collections, Reader's Digest employees, and the coming consolidation of the European Common Market in 1992. Initiated in 1987, the campaign is still going strong, spreading its message among employees as well as among business and advertising leaders.

Let Your Image Do Your Recruiting

A successful image program can also go a long way toward attracting new, quality workers. It says to potential recruits—both white collar and blue—that this is

Our vast global presence stems from the universal appeal of our products, which are published in the local language all over the world.

Reader's Digest, the world's most widely read magazine, is printed in 39 editions and 15 languages including Arabic, Chinese, Hindi and Korean. Every month more than 100 million people in every country in the world read our original articles and condensed selections from local and international sources.

Reader's Digest also ranks among the world's largest book publishers with annual sales of more than 40 million volumes in 10 languages. And we're one of the largest producers and global marketers of recorded music.

To succeed as a global publisher, you have to know your local markets, speak the local language and live the local customs. That's why every Reader's Digest product is a global best-seller—and that's worth a little flag-waving.

Reader's Digest.

We're a leading force in providing knowledge and entertainment to the world through magazine and book publishing, music and video products, travel and financial services. We also provide significant support for programs for youth, education, the arts and humanities, both directly and through the Reader's Digest Foundation.

Reader's Digest

We make a difference in 100 million lives worldwide.

Banner business.

Courtesy of The Readers' Digest Association.

Courtesy of The Readers' Digest Association.

a company worth looking at, a company known and respected by its peers, its industry, and by the public in general.

J.P. Morgan designs recruitment ads intentionally to look like their corporate series, creating a synergism. And Morgan's recruiters say that one of their most effective tools is a booklet of corporate ad reprints, which they update from time to time. International Paper, too, says that their own image program has definitely "improved college recruiting efforts."[5] And these are but two of the many companies, large and small, that recognize the value of a strong corporate image in attracting a steady flow of both clerical workers and management candidates.

MOBILIZE A TOTAL STRATEGY

Image advertising is but one way to tell the corporate story to your own or potential employees and to their communities. It's not the most direct, perhaps, but it is an effective method, and accomplishes a great deal more than merely impressing your people and their neighbors.

Like most advertising campaigns, an image series should be supported by a broad variety of other communications tools. Both employee relations and community relations programs utilize many media and techniques.

This book, of course, is about advertising; it isn't a manual on labor relations nor is it our task to explore and evaluate all the other aspects of employee relations. Suffice to list some of the more traditional internal communication methods such as house organs, newsletters, employee manuals and handbooks, annual reports, paycheck stuffers, exhibits, small and large meetings, memoranda, closed-circuit television and films, as well as external public relations. These all contribute to how an employee thinks of his or her company, how well he promotes it within his own personal circle and community, and how well the community receives the message.

In a recent interview, Thomas Haas of United Technologies commented on the advantages of total employee communications.

> There's a whole host of available methods, stemming from a need to communicate more and more with employees on every level. We definitely want to keep them informed as to the crucial part they play in all of this. For example, we're doing a lot more mailings to the home; before we release updates to the press, we send them to our employees.
>
> In return we have received letters from employees who thank us profusely for the television campaign because now they can explain and point

---

[5] "Never Underestimate . . ."

with pride to their part of the company and the specific job they do. One pointed out that now his wife and kids are more understanding of his role at the company and how the time he spends away from home or late at night contributes to corporate success.

Even before United Technologies launched their own recent image series, they did an employee focus campaign. Its emphasis was to highlight the important part individuals play in contributing to the success of the company, and how they work together to find solutions and meet customer demands. That particular campaign ran in the *Wall Street Journal,* but note that it *also* ran in all the hometown papers of United Technologies' various subsidiary businesses.

Over and above the support given corporate image, this local image advertising gets communities saying: "Gee, here's a company that cares about its employees and recognizes the fact that they are what contributes to its success." Says Haas, "That kind of thing pervades throughout the organization, and people start feeling better about the company."

A sense of pride is a fairly common employee reaction to well-conceived image advertising. The Travelers reports that their campaign acts positively on employee morale, and that they receive many unsolicited comments from employees to the effect: "I saw that TV spot and felt proud," or "Having seen the ads, people are impressed that I work for The Travelers."

Image Advertising Reflects Coors' Corporate Values

Coors Brewing Corporation also knows how to use image advertising to build community and employee relations. Employee wellness and professional growth, environmental progressiveness, and moderation in the use of their products are key interest areas for Coors' image advertising, but the single most important is the enhancement of community relations.

Coors' image ads have run in leading Colorado and national publications since 1986. Typical is this one on community relations, headlined: *"Coors Touches Us All."* Copy reads in part:

> Coors is making a difference. In the lives and economic security of its 10,000 employees and almost everyone else who lives in Colorado . . . more than 1,000 charitable, civic, educational and other organizations in our state received $3 million plus in contributions from Coors last year . . . Coors volunteers donated 34,000 hours of their own time . . . Coors is not just committed to making great beer. It's committed to making a great Colorado. For all of us.

Other ads continue the theme of company/employee/community relationships. Headlines like: "You don't have to make waves to make things happen" and

Courtesy of Coors Brewing Company.

"Can a company be healthy if its employees are not?" introduce ads on the story of the Coors volunteer organization called V.I.C.E. (Volunteers In Community Enrichment) and on the Coors Wellness Center, a state-of-the-art facility providing employees with a complete fitness center, medical screening and testing, and educational programs.

Coors understands that the three-way combination of company, employees, and community can be unbeatable, and they do much more than pay lip service to the concept.

Ashland Oil: Corporate Citizen

Another corporation that recognizes the principle of three-way communication is Ashland Oil. Ashland knows that as you need to keep employees informed about company products, services, and policies, so too you need to communicate thoroughly with your plant and facility communities. They should recognize your willingness to respond to local needs and interests. You have a vital stake in the health and prosperity of the towns you inhabit, as they have an obvious stake in the success and prosperity of your business. Lack of concern for community needs destroys corporate image.

Most corporations today are aware of the value of this relationship. Ashland Oil, in fulfilling its responsibilities as a corporate citizen, is particularly active in its communities. Through education and special programs, Ashland provides financial aid and leadership for many activities designed to improve the quality of life in areas where employees live.

Corporate regional advertising supports this program by focusing on the needs and importance of quality education and by encouraging students to stay in school. Financial assistance is provided to organizations involved in health and welfare, education, culture, youth, and civic improvement projects. Each year a number of major grants are offered by the company, making possible many community improvements.

Ashland management maintains direct involvement with community leaders, including public officials, other business executives, union leaders, clergy, educators, and ethnic and neighborhood leaders. Employees are encouraged to become involved with civic and social organizations and to volunteer time to a wide variety of community activities.

Other major forms of community relations include corporate philanthropy, support for the arts, plant and facility tours, and scholarships. All tend to enhance corporate image on the local level and beyond. All say to employees and community: "We're a concerned organization . . . we're a respected organization . . . we're an involved organization. You can be proud of us!"

Navistar: People Make the Company Function

The story of Navistar—the development and promotion of a new identity for International Harvester—has already been detailed in Chapter 3. At this point, however, we'll review the change's effect on their employees and communities. Says John McDonald, Navistar's director of communications: "We looked closely at the psychological impact a new identity would have on our employees. They were comfortable with International Harvester, and we had to create an environment in which they could become comfortable with Navistar.

"It's people who make any company function. Taking that simple wisdom at face value, we chose our employees as the first audience to receive information regarding our new identity."

In preparing their plan, Navistar set up five criteria to be met in making the announcement to their own people. These were:

1. Introduce the new identity in a dramatic fashion.

2. The message should come directly from the chairman and president.

3. All employees should be involved simultaneously.

4. The message should be clear, concise, and visual.

5. The introduction had to reflect the company's rebirth.

"To do all of these things," says McDonald, "we proposed a live broadcast, by satellite transmission, to all of our major facilities throughout North America. For the first time, our chairman and president would address all of our employees live!"

Navistar management established a network of 25 employee contacts, located at each company location to oversee the coordination of technical facilities, the distribution of literature and promotional materials, and the gathering of employees to viewing areas.

On the day of the announcement, Navistar's two top executives spoke to the employees about the change. In addition to these executive speeches there were two specially produced videotapes highlighting both the new identity and the value of the employees. The entire presentation itself was videotaped for the benefit of second- and third-shift workers at various locations.

When employees returned to their work stations, they received information kits containing literature designed to further explain and position the company's new identity. There were also special mementos such as hats, pins, and bumper stickers—simple gifts but very important in encouraging the employees to feel a part of their "new" company.

Another major phase of Navistar's communications plan centered around a very intensive, high-profile advertising campaign which began the day after the announcement. Like other aspects of the announcement, the ad campaign was very visually oriented and utilized network television, radio, and print publications such as *Business Week, Forbes, Fortune, Time,* the *Wall Street Journal,* the *New York Times,* and *USA Today.*

Although the ads were aimed primarily at general business and financial publics, they were designed with all Navistar constituencies in mind. Certain ads, including one appropriately called ''Neighbors,'' were run in newspapers serving towns and cities where the company had plants or other facilities. The intent of this particular ad was to raise the identity comfort level of employees—and their families, friends, and neighbors—while thanking them for a job well done.

Employees Are Always a Target

Whatever your corporate image mission, your own employees belong right up there with other target audiences. If they don't understand and have faith in company plans it isn't very likely that others will either.

But if your employees are well informed about your company, its products and services, and its future, they will serve as a good example, attracting new employees on all levels and helping contribute to cooperative attitudes in company towns. And that can mean a great deal to a profitable bottom line.

CHAPTER NINE

One Important Reminder:
We Are Not Alone

■ So far this text has examined some compelling reasons for employing corporate image advertising and has posited why its use grows so rapidly. We have covered seven major missions and set forth certain guidelines and rules for achieving image goals. Much recent and pertinent case study material has shown how a number of the nation's corporations and banks have approached their own image problems and solved their own image needs.

Seven Missions of Image Advertising

Without attempting any major review, perhaps we should at least list those seven missions again:

1. To build public awareness and acceptance, and establish a more favorable market position.

2. To redefine your corporation after a merger, takeover, acquisition, or name change.

3. To pre-sell target markets to support product marketing.

4. To influence shareholders and the financial community.

5. To establish your company's position on timely issues.

6. To assist in the management of a crisis situation.

7. To attract and hold quality employees, while creating a cooperative environment in plant communities.

These missions may be employed individually or in countless combinations. Much depends, of course, upon the needs and perceptions of your various target publics.

Six Guidelines for a Successful Image Campaign

We have also covered six basic guidelines—concepts which, when followed, can greatly improve the chances that your image campaign will succeed. These are:

1. *Perception* is what counts; it's not necessarily the reality of a situation but what your target audience *considers* to be reality that creates corporate image.

2. *Direction* for an image campaign should be established by the top person—usually the CEO. He or she is the only one who understands the company from all viewpoints and can employ personal involvement toward reconciling conflicts between divisions and departments, keep the campaign going on track, and find the necessary budget to get the job done.

3. *Know thyself.* You've got to know who you are before you can decide where you're going. You've got to know whether you really need an image campaign at all; know your company's current image and be able to project what it should be; know when your company has reached its goal and how to maintain the new image. How? Research. Before, during, and after any image program.

4. *Focus:* do you know *who* you are trying to reach? The better you recognize and understand your audience(s), the better you can alter their perceptions of your company.

5. *Creativity.* What will your campaign say to its target publics? What single specific appeal will best cut through the clutter, be remembered and acted upon? Study your audience; they are the only ones who can provide the answer.

6. *Consistency.* The execution of your advertising, or the *how* of it, involves not only ad theme and quality, but also consistency and continuity of exposure. No matter how well focused and creative, without consistency your entire investment may be wasted.

But how can you be sure your advertising has the appeal and excitement to make itself heard? There is so much advertising out there, competing hotly for your public's attention. Why should the reader or viewer pay particular notice and attention to *your* message?

Hopefully your ads will contain some spark of creative genius to penetrate the general indifference that so often greets corporate advertising. In other words, *how* you say something can be just as important as *what* you say. President Kennedy, when he went to West Berlin, might have simply said, ''I want to help you.'' He didn't. He said, ''Ich bin ein Berliner.'' And that thought, that turn of phrase, became an international byword.

Creative genius, of course, cannot be planned. The people responsible for your advertising either have it or they don't, and, frankly, many advertising people don't. That's why it's so critical to select your advertising agency with care. Unfortunately, not all agencies have creative geniuses in residence.

FOUR CREATIVE STEPS

We can't guarantee that you'll find genius at your agency, but we have provided four simple steps that can lead to creative excellence when followed by experienced, professional copywriters and artists:

1. Keep your advertising simple, to the point, and honest. Never insult the reader's intelligence.

2. Avoid self-congratulation. The marketplace isn't concerned with how well you can pat yourself on the back.

3. Sink your advertising's roots deep into your products, your capabilities,

your services, or your policies—and conceive it from the point of view of your target publics.

4. Above all, make your ads interesting—attention grabbing, attention holding. This is where it's particularly nice to have that genius to call upon!

Anyone can make up rules, of course. The trick is to get them to work effectively together toward the goal. That's why these certain concepts are especially valuable. They have been put to the test over and over by many of the nation's most experienced and talented practitioners of corporate advertising. They work.

Even so, they may not be enough.

ONE BASIC RULE

For all of their value, such guidelines are not always sufficient in today's changing and globally oriented marketplace. One special commandment must be added to the list: Never forget that we are not alone. Other countries, with their own economies, business structures, and societies, are breathing hard on our necks. And in all too many cases they have already caught up or passed us.

Your company's sales may be exclusively within our own borders. Your financing may be 100 percent homegrown. You may not even have to import raw materials or parts. But foreign nations, foreign businesses, foreign investments now bear heavily upon your success—not only your immediate success but the very future of your business.

It's a rare corporation of any size that can exist for long in total isolation from today's international events. The world has shrunk too much. The marketplace has grown too competitive. Corporate communications have become far too complex, and as companies compete more and more in countries far removed from their own, the range of communication has expanded markedly.

Integrate Social Concerns with Economic Issues

Companies that do compete successfully overseas have learned that the multinational must be broad enough in its outlook to know the differences, the nuances, required of its corporate communications in responding to the many influences of many public perceptions in many places. Almost limitless impacts, all interrelated—economic, political, social—work dramatically to alter business situations abroad.

Ethyl Corporation is one internationally oriented company that looks ahead to inevitable changes. Ethyl Corporation's Harwood Ritter underscores this global perspective:

> The centralized efforts in Europe to consolidate its 12 member states into a Common Market are making it easier to establish social as well as economic guidelines for the conduct of business.
>
> Unlike the long evolution of rules that have developed for business between countries in other parts of the world, Europeans are collectively building a planned business community with a social conscience. The business guidelines that are evolving conspicuously integrate social concerns such as environment, community, and education with economic issues. As a result, companies wishing to conduct business in the Common Market must be sensitive to these same concerns with their actions, and with their communications.
>
> Although companies in the United States have not ignored social responsibility, they are not used to communicating economic and social topics as a homogeneous issue. From all indications, greater continuity of purpose with all communications will not be simply a desirable corporate objective, but a necessary element for business success in the European Community. What's more, it is very possible that the ideas coming out of Europe will be adopted by other nations or groups of nations.

J.P. MORGAN SPEAKS THE LOCAL LANGUAGE

One sensitive approach to international image is employed by J.P. Morgan. When they advertise overseas, it's in the language of the country in which the ads appear. Though research has shown that better than 90 percent of their primary target audiences in Europe, for example, reads and understands English, Morgan prefers to talk to a French CEO in French, a German controller in German, an Italian businessman in Italian, and so forth. They feel this emphasizes the indigenous nature of Morgan offices abroad while also underscoring the bank's internationality.

Bruce Roberts, Morgan vice president, adds: "We [also] set out to maintain consistency in the graphic appearance of all of our ads, including those run overseas. When we prepare an ad to announce the opening of a new office or a move to a new location, the corporate format is used. And when an office in a particular country wants an ad to describe its capabilities in that market, [this ad too] is designed to bear the distinctive Morgan look."

A single basic format, always in the proper language and context, respects local needs and says, "This is a J.P. Morgan message."

Unisys: Not Just a U.S. Marketplace

Another corporation employing a unifying ad format in global markets is Unisys. Formed in 1986 by the merger of the Burroughs and Sperry Corporations, Unisys' first mission for its corporate advertising was to establish the new name throughout the world—to create an identity and a positioning that looks forward, that trades some of the past of the old corporations for the future, worldwide growth of a new, stronger competitor.

That mission still exists today, but has been expanded to include three key attributes of the company:

1. that it provides the customer with a wide choice of products;

2. that it offers the customer total flexibility; and

3. that UNISYS people are service-committed for the customer's satisfaction.

Unisys strives for a global image, one as valid in Europe, Asia, and South America as it is in the United States. Robert O'Leary, corporate director of advertising, points out: ''We have a single unifying format for all corporate advertising throughout the world. Overseas we have European, Asian, and South American organizations, and each individual country has a general management in place.

''Through our agency, Young & Rubicam, we supply these organizations with the ad format and a series of strategic messages from which they create their own ad copy. We also give them the typeface and the general look they should adhere to. And they all use our tag line, 'We make it happen,' and the logo in proper position (see illustrations). This consistency is important because it assures that the same corporate image is reflected in whatever part of the world we are doing business.''

Operate from a Common Communications Platform

Bull Worldwide Information Systems, formerly Honeywell-Bull, approaches a global marketplace with a brand new identity. The original mission of its image program was just to get the new name established. A second phase adds more substance about the company, i.e., experience, stature, posture, point of view, etc.

As of this writing, Bull Worldwide is looking to enter still another phase of its image advertising. Mark Minkin, director of corporate advertising, reports: ''My current role is to get about 20 key countries pretty much pulling in the same direction. Positioning the company the same way, positioning our services, products, solutions in the same way, and operating from a common communications platform.'' In other words, integrating such pertinent markets as Italy, the United Kingdom, France, and Germany, as well as the United States, under a single communications theme aimed at the same target audiences of CEOs, CIOs, and GIOs [a Bull Worldwide term—Global Information Officers].

In each country Bull Worldwide buys the principal local media—leading dailies and industry and business magazines. Schedules are structured in a similar way, and target audiences are pretty much the same from country to country. In addition to this indigenous media, they buy an overall corporate schedule, too, in the *International Herald Tribune, Time, Newsweek,* and similar publications, generally printed in English.

In trying to understand better the new, global role of corporate advertising, Bull Worldwide conducts active research at both a local U.S. level and on a worldwide basis. This latter, although commissioned and funded out of France, is structured to measure the company's awareness and perception factors on a country-by-country basis.

Meet the Competition Head-On

The need for global awareness includes a good deal more, of course, than merely developing overseas customers for U.S. products and services. It also means competing successfully here at home with determined foreign marketers. It means protecting U.S. markets, which for years were pretty much our private domain, from a flood of cheaper, often better-made goods. In the mid-1980s, for example, the general feeling was that the Japanese had sounded the death knell for the U.S. semiconductor business. In 1986, Texas Instruments (TI) was the only major semiconductor supplier still in the DRAM (dynamic random-access memory) chips business. The press was proclaiming that the semiconductor worldwide business battle had in large part been lost by the United States and won by the Japanese.

Texas Instruments management, at that time led by Semiconductor Group President Bill Sick, believed it was important for TI to stay in the DRAM business. It was his thesis that DRAMs are technology drivers; advanced technologies for all ICs (integrated circuits) are refined in the DRAM arena. The skills and disciplines developed in the high-volume memory business are applied across TI's entire product spectrum.

This results in significant technological benefits to customers dealing with IC suppliers active in the DRAM business. It also positions TI as a technology

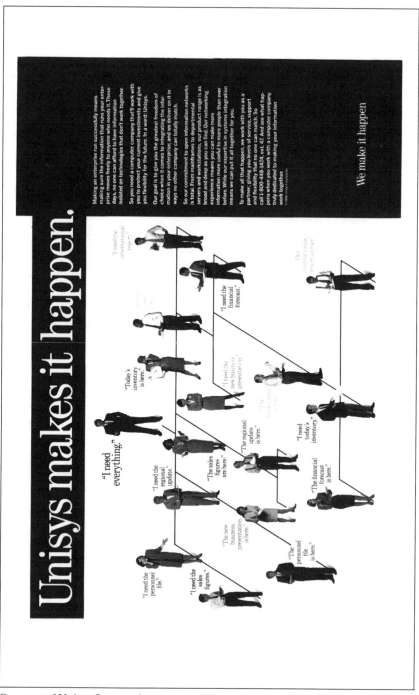

Courtesy of Unisys Corporation.

Courtesy of Unisys Corporation.

leader and allows them a platform from which to discuss the issue in a context broader than simply DRAMs.

At this same time, decision-making levels were rising in the TI semiconductor customer base. As ICs have driven the ability for manufacturers to develop differentiated products, the decisions regarding IC supplier selection have, in many cases, risen to policy-level corporate management. Says Ed Morrett, TI's manager of market communications, "Technology is fast becoming a 'bet your company' decision."

Morrett continues, "That's why our MegaChip Technologies image campaign was born. This advertising allows us to talk to the upper tier of business management about issues of interest to them. The term *MegaChip* was not conceived to designate any specific product or device, but rather to denote a sense of technological strength, and to provide a vehicle by which Texas Instruments can discuss nonproduct issues.

"MegaChip Technologies has evolved to mean anything that TI does to serve the customer better, whether it be technology or service oriented. TI's promise is to 'help customers get to market faster with a more competitive product.' "

When this campaign rolled out in September 1986, *Time* had already prepared an article covering its view that the Americans had given up the semiconductor industry to the Japanese. Upon seeing the first eight-page MegaChip insertion *Time* scrapped the pending article, and the resulting piece was one of hope and positive reporting.

As the campaign evolved, growing evidence that primary customer interests now included more than mere technology indicated that advertising strategy should move "closer to the customer." A Customer Success Profile, or case history approach, was developed and implemented in 1989 (see illustrations).

Formal research as well as conversations with customers support TI's belief that its image advertising helped save an important market for the company, even though they were competing with the supposedly "unbeatable" Japanese. Says Morrett: "We feel the campaign has been successful not only in the area of VLSI semiconductors, but has also improved the profile of Texas Instruments in its ability to meet increasing customer requirements."

Corporate Image and the National Image

The trend today is to look to image advertising to open doors in overseas markets and help stem the tide of invading marketers in the U.S. But whether you are selling overseas or merely competing at home, corporate image is only part of today's solution. Increasingly our *national* image makes a substantial contribution to your success—or failure. The way our nation is perceived by overseas businesses and their governments reflects directly on U.S. corporate images. It has a great deal to do with how those countries will compete here and how we can compete with them abroad.

You need only read the headlines. Japan's economic invasion of the United States, never-ending crisis, even war, in the oil-rich Middle East, the coming 1992 consolidation of the European Common Market, the astounding effects of *glasnost* on the Communist bloc nations, our own staggering national debt and trade deficit—don't these leave their marks on the national economy and thus on your business? Do not our reactions and responses to such situations contribute to our nation's image abroad as well as at home? to your industry's image? to your company's image?

Where once the United States stood tall and proud, the world's leading industrial nation and major supplier to the free world, we now take a backseat more often than not. Much of our major real estate—including such national landmarks as Rockefeller Center and Aspen—is now owned and controlled by foreign capital. And the balance of trade has shifted so greatly that instead of supplying other nations we now buy from them.

Doesn't this national image affect your corporate image overseas? Doesn't it bear on how your overseas competitors go to market here?

Reinvent the American Experience

What can we do? Listen to Robin Bergstrom, an editor with *Production* magazine:

> We do what we never had to do. We reinvent the American experience. Accept the premise that America may, indeed, be only a state of mind, a place not bound by the limits of geography; may be, in fact, an idea toward which we are constantly moving.
>
> Change some of the rules, alter some of the structures, forge new forms and shapes. Reinvent who we are in such a fashion that we may become who we must to survive. We reinvent who we are in light of our global neighbors and with a regard to an unyielding future.[1]

---

[1]"Hard Times, Parts 1 and 2: Do Not Go Gentle and Rage, Rage Against The Dying Of The Light," Robin P. Bergstrom, Editor-at-Large *Production,* The Magazine of Manufacturing Management, July and August 1990.

Courtesy of Texas Instruments.

Courtesy of Texas Instruments.

Isn't this the same as creating a shiny new, expanded national image? But how do we go about that?

Bergstrom continues: "We test the mettle of some of our long-held traditions and institutions, [and] dismantle some of the labyrinthine bureaucracy. And the American learning experience—which must go beyond the classroom and address students college bound and noncollege bound, embrace training and retraining—is a good place to begin.

"We must remember: human capital is our most significant competitive tool. This is not merely true in an age of high technology. High technology, in fact, *demands,* a more numerate, literate, and articulate workforce. More than strong hands, the era of the microchip requires astute minds. If you don't believe this, ask our international competition."

Yes, ask our international competition. They understand that human capital *is* the most important competitive tool. The quality and capabilities of the work force predetermine the success not only of a corporate image but of the very business itself.

THE RIGHT THING TO DO

A growing number of U.S. companies believe this—Ashland Oil, for one. That's why in 1983 they initiated a multi-million-dollar educational support campaign as the basis for their corporate advertising. J. Dan Lacy, Ashland's vice president for corporate communications, has said: "A company's efforts to maintain public acceptance is a continuing process. Business leaders must demonstrate a sense of moral and social responsibility and play a sincere and meaningful role in the community if they are to gain public support."

"In other words, we've got to make a difference and affect the community in a positive way through products or services. And we have to do it in a way that says, 'My company isn't doing this just to increase sales. My company isn't doing this just to improve its image. My company is doing this because it is the right thing to do, and we are in a position to do it.' "

This is the message behind Ashland Oil's commitment to education, a commitment that goes back to the 1930s, when company founder Paul G. Blazer began to cultivate responsible corporate attitudes among his employees. Today, Blazer's beliefs—that the development of well-educated men and women is vital to the nation and to industry; that the need for *quality* education is equally vital; that there is an important need for the interaction of education and business on all levels—continue to live on and prosper. Lacy continues:

> In 1983 the National Commission on Excellence in Education published a
> report that criticized America's educational system and called for sweeping

changes in both policies and attitudes. Statistics cited were chilling. Some 23 million Americans were functionally illiterate . . . illiteracy among minority youths was as high as 40 percent . . . average achievement of high school students was the lowest in 26 years . . . etc., etc., etc.

Between the national concern caused by this document and the Blazer traditions, Ashland needed no prodding. We stepped up an already sizable support of education and devoted our corporate advertising budget to increasing public awareness of the importance of and need for quality education.

We realized in order to change the future, the specific targets of the present had to be defined and attacked.

A Four-Pronged Approach

Ashland's approach to the educational problem includes four major components:

1. *"Teachers Change Lives,"* Ashland Oil's current corporate advertising effort that recognizes teachers' important role in society and focuses on how they impact the lives of at-risk students.

2. *"A Day on Campus"* provides one-day visits to college campuses for students in fourth through ninth grades in West Virginia and Kentucky. The program exposes students to college and encourages them to dream and discover how they, too, might attend.

3. *"Critical Factors"* is a 12-minute audio-visual program for elementary schools, discussing the skills of reading, mathematics, communications, and thinking. It challenges children to dream about their future.

4. *The AdCouncil Dropout Prevention Campaign.* Ashland provided a previous year's promotion on student dropout prevention to the AdCouncil for national distribution, funding the reproduction of print and television ads. This is the only time the AdCouncil has adapted a corporate campaign for use as a national PSA program.

Even though every year Ashland strives to improve their efforts, they realize the battle will not be won quickly or easily. Much is yet to be done, with today's statistics as alarming as those reported in 1983.

Today statistics show that of 3.8 million 18-year-old Americans in 1988, at least 700,000 had dropped out of school and another 700,000, who graduated, couldn't read well enough to be called literate—illiteracy among minority students is *still* as high as 40 percent. In standardized tests between 1983 and 1986,

American students came in last in biology, eleventh in chemistry, and ninth in physics among students from only 13 countries.

Corporate Responsibility

Lacy concludes: "At Ashland Oil we believe corporate America must make commitments—real, long-term commitments, based on real values—to gain respect from the public. We have a responsibility. There are thousands of children out there, listening . . . If we can encourage them to stay in school, if we can foster within them a desire to learn, if we can help them realize dreams, then we must not hesitate . . . It is an investment in the future.

"As our Chairman and CEO, John R. Hall, has said: 'Education is one of our greatest national resources because it has the power to build the foundation of our prosperity.' "

Ashland's is obviously a strong image program, an advocacy that is hard to challenge. But is education really *that* important to our national economy, our nation's future? Let's see what happened when the 18-year-olds referred to above hit the work force.

- Productivity losses caused by poorly trained workers and remedial training cost industry about $25 billion a year—a cost our closest international competitors do not have.

- It is estimated that as much as a quarter of the U.S. labor force is illiterate, costing business over $6 billion annually in lost productivity.

- Every fifth person now hired by American industry is both illiterate and innumerate.

The depressing statistics are seemingly endless. Robin Bergstrom notes: "What we are talking about is a self-induced national bankruptcy: the loss of international competitiveness in nearly every American industrial sector through suicidal human resource debasement. We are on a collision course with our own future. We simply will not—and do not—have the cadre of literate, competent, skilled workers needed to sustain us for the remainder of this century and on into the next as a serious global contender."

It is not our purpose here to investigate the many aspects of the course of national education, with all of its problems and possible solutions. That can be left for other writers, other books. It *is* our intention, however, to point out the alarming effect education—or the lack of it—is having on our ability to compete successfully in today's ever changing global marketplace.

This book is about corporate image advertising and how it assists individual corporations in going to market successfully. But we cannot ignore the value of national image in the success of business and industry both abroad and at home. No matter how well conceived and executed, corporate images are increasingly dependent upon our nation's image in the eyes of other nations. National educational levels represent only a part of our nation's total image, of course. But it is decidedly an important part.

Nor can every corporation approach its image requirements in the same manner as Ashland Oil, although many other companies, as well as individual businesspeople, do support an improved quality of education in one way or another.

But this couldn't be a better time for corporate leaders and other thinking Americans to attend to the thorny problems involved in changing a national image, and education is just one good place to start.

GE—
"We Bring Good Things to Life"

■ A conversation between the author, Richard Costello, GE, and Dick White (formerly GE account supervisor, at BBDO) about the "We Bring Good Things to Life" campaign: how it started, how it evolved, and how it was sold internally and externally.

Gregory: I'd like to ask about the atmosphere before the campaign was launched. Did Jack Welch just come in as chairman?

Costello: No, it started before he was chairman—he was at that point a vice-chairman. He was one of several individuals who was in the running for chairmanship, his responsibility was at that point what we call the consumer sector—it no longer organizationally exists—but at that time was a conglomeration of all our consumer businesses. He found an organization which from a business point of view was doing OK but not great. It had all of these different products and services. I mean we had hundreds of different product lines targeted at the consumer. Each division was kind of doing its own thing, each had its own advertising agency, and often its own advertising slogan, and none of it worked together.

White: Before '78 when Reg Jones created the sectors, GE was sort of the mother of decentralization—going from a highly centralized to a highly decentralized operation. They had 43 separate business units operating independently. In '78 they reorganized the company into five, later seven, sectors to try to come into a middle ground between over centralization and over decentralization.

The consumer products services sector, of which Jack Welch was the first head, consisted at that point of these five groups—housewares, major appliances, lamps, televisions, air conditioners, and those are the major product lines within each of those units—so we had 21 major product lines, about 100–plus subsidiary lines and $5 billion in sales represented by that overall sector. But there was really no relationship between one group and another in terms of even the way they were presenting themselves to the consumer in their marketing efforts.

Costello: Each product line had its own thing—they tended to be driven by the ad manager who picked his own agency and his divisional manager who wanted to have his own little thing. There was a committee that used to meet and coordinate, but that just meant that everyone would meet and say what they were doing and go back to their cubbyholes and do it. So there was very little coordination.

White: The bigger issue was that the head of each of these units and the individual sub-units were being judged on how they did individually and not on how the rest of the sector did, or even how the corporation did. The impact of that, at least in terms of advertising, was a real concern. Each SBU, that's Strategic Business Unit, marketed and advertised its products independently. There were 32 separate advertising campaigns, most of which were addressed to some portion of the consumer market.

Gregory: What was the nature of these campaigns?

White: They were highly fragmented. There were no interactive elements, no GE focus, no commonality, the advertising generally concentrated on individual products, or on parts of GE rather than on GE as a whole.

Gregory: How did that affect your image in the marketplace?

Costello: We had some terrific values, quality, solidity, reliability. We were rock solid, safe, a supplier of those goods and services. But, our image lacked in some areas. We weren't seen as particularly innovative in the consumer goods business. Our image was not seen as particularly appropriate to consumer electronics in particular which was the most innovative part of business. And we were seen as old-fashioned and fuddy-duddy in our design, style, and approach, which, in the late '70s and early '80s as the baby boomers were coming into the market, wasn't an appropriate image to appeal to that younger group. Yet we knew just from the demographic work there was going to be a boom in the '80s driven by a demography that was going to help us in all of our household goods. So from the market point of view and the image point of view we decided we needed to revitalize our image. We were under-optimizing our resources by having them fragmented. Those were things that Welch concluded.

Gregory: So what did Welch do next?

White: He went to Y&R and BBDO and said he was really concerned about this whole issue of consumer perception and GE's imagery and by the fact that we were not getting the right leverage out of our reputation and out of the position we really enjoyed in the consumer's home. We had to get a handle on the magnitude of that problem . . . how serious it was, what its various aspects were, and what, if anything, we should do about it. When we say ''if anything'' we mean it may be a problem, but if it's not hurting us it may not be worth the money to solve it. But if it is hurting us, let's find out to what extent it is and how important that is and how much it would be worth to put something in there to fix it. So the challenge to Y&R and BBDO was to get down into their research, determine how GE looked to the individual out there—to try to get a quantitative fix on it and then come in with a recommended way of dealing with it.

The two agencies were given that assignment in February and were supposed to come back in early April with a diagnosis and preliminary prescription as to what should be done. Based on GE's acceptance of their preliminary work, the agencies were going to come up with creative and media approaches to deal with the problem. Whichever agency won would get everything. Whichever agency lost would lose everything. So it was a major effort. We went through all of their research, did a lot of our own, and went through other available research in terms of the whole corporate advertising issue, which is why as I remember there wasn't much available at that time.

Costello: At this point it was kind of unheard of that anyone who had this diversity of product lines would even attempt to do this. I think candidly both BBDO and Y&R thought this was a crazy idea. That was my impression from discussions I had with people at the time.

Gregory: What did the agencies find?

White: Awareness levels across all markets were generally lower than GE's own market position, which means they were doing better in the market than they were doing in terms of share of mind. The overall profile was good but not great, dependable but not state of the art, reliable but not exciting, functional but not stylish, mass but not class, generalists not specialists, a follower not a leader, slow to react, not in touch and not responsive. A lot of this was a function of what they were not saying about themselves, and was a function too of the various specialists that they were competing with in each of these major product categories. It was bad enough in terms of where they wanted to go with their businesses, that they wanted to do something about it. But they had to bring some order out of it.

Gregory: Were both agencies still in the running?

Costello: Yes. Both agencies presented, I believe, two campaigns apiece. Welch at the presentation picked "We bring good things to life," which was developed by BBDO's Phil Dusenberry, Ted Sand, and Dennis Burger, who were the key creative people in that team. They developed the line, the music, the concept of showing the diversity of the product line. How it affected people's lives, kind of day-to-day and every-hour-of-every-day. I think the power of it was that it was a catchy and memorable line, reinforced by catchy and memorable music, but I also think it was a clever thing that they did . . . There really is no claim in it at all, but what it did was point out to people in a way that had not been apparent to them, but which consumers knew, like "Oh yeah, I do have those things in the kitchen, and they do light the house." And it reminded them of all those things and other things they were less aware of that they had buried in the back of their minds. People brought GE forward from the recessess of their minds to something more relevant and tangible day to day.

Gregory: How did the creative concept evolve?

White: We wanted to be distinctive. The line that says "GE Makes Your Life Better" was a big snore. It wasn't going to be what we said that would make us distinctive; it was going to be how we said it. It's executional . . . You can't look at the concept by itself because it's not going to be what impacts your house. You're not going to find something that's going to be intellectually gripping. We had to exploit the fact that GE is in everybody's home—it's like wallpaper, they stopped noticing it. Find a way of talking to people that will get them not so much market share, but help share. Working for GE to raise people's consciousness of GE as a helping hand, if you will. It took a long time to come to grips with that and frankly I don't think anybody fully understood until we saw some initial creative treatments. The idea of GE helping to make your life better, helping to make it more pleasant, less of a hassle, at least starting at that point. That's what essentially happened where we talk about basing the advertising on the understanding of GE's role in people's daily lives. The advertising promotes that GE does more things for more people . . . helps improve the quality of their lives . . . brings good things to life.

After a major creative exploratory that went on for about six to eight weeks, we then presented two campaigns to Jack Welch some time in early June. The same day that Y&R presented. Y&R went through much the same intellectual exercise we did. They gave us the go-ahead the next day to produce it and get it on the air by the week after Labor Day, which was unbelievable because we had to not only create the corporate advertising, we had to sectorize all of the divisional advertising, some of which we weren't handling, because at that point we did not have majors or air-conditioning. So we had about 200 people working on this business that summer, with about three different creative teams out there shooting commercials, and doing end modifications and everything.

Gregory: So BBDO won the pitch. How did "We bring good things to life" then evolve into a campaign?

White: What we suggested was a multi-tier program, starting with a sector-wide umbrella campaign which would establish GE's brand image as a platform, a theme, a look, and a concept that we cut across all of their consumer markets. This, feeding down into the individual product programs that were being undertaken by majors, lamps, TV, air-conditioning and housewares, which would establish the concept. This platform, with the individual product programs or campaigns translating that brand image concept, theme, and look into product-specific advertising for the individual markets, would then feed into their collateral programs.

Costello: The businesses were encouraged by Welch to use the same slogan in their product advertising which was developed by a variety of agencies. There was some resistance but that very quickly melted away. Even old ads that had been running without a slogan were changed over to that piece of music and that little tag at the end "We bring good things to life." Everything got changed. That was introduced in the fourth quarter of 1979.

For the first time we tried to coordinate media schedules more effectively and encouraged the businesses to put all of their buying together and overlaid that with the sector money so we had more clout. It also happened to be the Winter Olympics that year in Lake Placid and we bought air time at discount rates because they were undersold and that got terrific ratings—remember the hockey team won and all that? It got great ratings. Bringing the money together, using one good theme line, and pretty effective creative work, plus getting some high visibility media—very suddenly in that quarter GE got noticed.

Courtesy of General Electric.

Gregory: How did you sell the campaign internally?

White: Because of the geographical dispersion of their units they just never talked to each other. Majors was in Louisville, audio was in Syracuse, small appliances was in Bridgeport, TV was in Portsmith, VA, and there was just no connection. So GE workers tended to say, "Hey, I work for GE majors." There was certainly no wholistic feel about consumers sector, and it was important that they be educated to realize that what a consumer felt about GE small appliances was heavily impacted by what they felt about GE ranges or GE TV, and if they were having trouble with their range they were not going to trust a GE TV. So qualitative performance issues coming out of audio or TV was very important to the other partners of the sector.

Gregory: Was it difficult to get that message across?

White: Frankly, everybody was so literal in those days. Marketing and advertising guys were really very functional, they said either GE dishwashers make your dishes cleaner, or do them faster, or with less noise, using less energy. These were all very important functional benefits, but we were missing an ultimate end benefit. It was very difficult, excruciatingly difficult, to come to grips with this intellectually. We sat there all day, at night we went home and came back the next day and said, "What have we got?"

Gregory: But you came up with a real winner with "We bring good things to life." It *is* much more humanistic than the previous corporate campaign which used the theme "Progress is our most important product."

Costello: And the executions are all driven that way. One continuity from day one to today is that the orientation has always been benefits. If you take the line "We bring good things to life" the emphasis is on *life* not on *things*. And it's been on benefits rather than our products. We try to insert our products in a way that shows how they pay off, but what we've tried to avoid as much as we can is the product-feature oriented advertising. It has more to do with what is the ultimate end benefit, even if that means to some degree doing generic advertising. We find that kind of advertising positions you as a leader anyway—most of the best advertising is generic to begin with.

In the fall of '79, interestingly, "Progress For People" was still running as a corporate campaign. Welch became chairman about 18 months later (early '81) and quickly realized the campaign "We bring good things to life" had really achieved some momentum and he said, "Why don't we just use that everywhere?" And so by the fall of '81 a corporate campaign was developed which broadened the idea of bringing good things to life in the kitchen and the home to literally every aspect of people's lives. We had commercials on aircraft engines—how they brought people together—on our medical equipment—how

Courtesy of General Electric.

it helped make you healthier without going into invasive surgery—and on a variety of other high technology products.

White: So by the fall of '81 what had started as a consumer product driven campaign became a corporate statement which encompassed the whole company. It has pretty much remained that way ever since.

Gregory: Over the years, what was the mix between a consumer message *vs.* a strictly corporate message in your corporate advertising?

Costello: The balance of spending between what we call corporate messages and what we call consumer messages has shifted over time. I'd say in the early years it was 70 to 80 percent consumer products and 20 percent corporate or non-consumer products. As Welch changed the portfolio of the company over that period of time he shifted it from about 20 percent of our company being consumer goods in 1980 to about eight or nine percent in consumer goods today.

As that shift occurred, the message emphasis shifted to 50–50 between non-consumer and consumer product messages focussed primarily on appliances and lighting. And in some years it's almost been 60/40 in favor of corporate-type messages. The reason for that is twofold: we found that often a message for a CAT scan can have terrific impact on the consumer community. The concept of selling high-quality, reliability, and technology transcends what product you actually are showing or demonstrating. Often we have more exciting stories in the non-consumer businesses, and they can help our business among consumers when they believe they can go out and buy a refrigerator tomorrow and that it will be a good refrigerator. We found often that the non-consumer products have terrific stories and a lot of leverage in building the impression of the company and what the trademark stands for.

Gregory: What other audiences are you reaching?

Costello: Our other objective is to try and get audiences other than consumers, particularly investors and the business community, to understand and know about our non-consumer goods and services. Either because they can buy them, or we feel they might drive up the stock prices. So, as time goes on the balance of messages has shifted, and also the media has shifted. We were originally very heavily into prime-time television. The shift really occurred in the late '80s dramatically. Our presence in prime time television dropped off substantially. We're now a larger presence in off-prime day parts, particularly information programming, with more upscale demographics generally. The use of cable and of PBS has also increased substantially. It doesn't mean we're off prime time altogether. But our overall corporate spending has shifted from selling consumer goods to selling to a broad array of publics our reputation and our image as a company, in the broader sense of the word. We're trying to reach you. Whether you're a legislator at the local or national level, whether you're a person in the Pentagon buying our defense equipment, whether you're an investor on Wall Street or you're a buyer in Ford Motor Company, or you're a consumer buying light bulbs. So the emphasis has shifted substantially and it's become more a classic kind of a corporate campaign. We still use that slogan throughout.

Gregory: Do you measure all those various audiences?

Costello: We have measured and continue to measure the consumer audience and a business decision-maker audience. We have also occasionally measured the security analysts and portfolio manager audience, but that's more on an on-again-off-again basis, depending on need. We have never measured the political decision-making audience. We get good feedback on that from our lobbyists. We have a lot of direct contact with them. But our two biggest study groups are consumers—a general population measure—and then we have an on-going study of what we call business decision makers which would be anyone from a purchasing agent up to a VP of a company.

Gregory: How did you know you had a winner when the campaign broke for "We bring good things to life"?

White: In the first two years, unaided advertising slogan awareness went up to 36 percent which was pretty terrific. People could relate to it. Brand awareness

GE Brand Awareness by Product Group		
	Prior to launch %	Two years later %
Major Appliances	24	32
Television	8	14
Housewares	35	38
Audio	26	34
Room Air Conditioning	19	24
Lamps	42	53

Source: GE Tracking Study.

Courtesy of General Electric.

by product line showed gains in every major product category of the period. The brand awareness figures are reflective of the dominant sort of position that the products enjoy in the market—lamps, with a 53 percent share of the business, had a 42 percent brand awareness to start with, for example.

We also did photo-sort research, which was a special technique which related the GE image to the image of various people in terms of trying to get a fix on their perceptions.

The impact of the campaign emotionally on the company was immense. The commercials were very different, they were very human—when we showed the commercials people would literally break down and cry. There was a warmth to them and a humanity to them and it was really GE helping people celebrate their lives. The further we got into the campaign the better we were able to play with that and make it really work in very improbable situations.

Gregory: It must have been difficult to accomplish considering the enormous range of GE products that you eventually needed to incorporate into the campaign.

White: One of the key problems was to make the commercials believable as a slice of life, etc., when you had to load them up with quite a lot of product. I think they did a great job. The consumer sector program started in '79 and was having its impact. By '81 they saw the equity that was building and I think everybody felt that you could take that concept of making your life better and apply it corporately, even though it seemed to be a stretch initially. When I say a stretch, you're dealing with a company that's making atomic reactors, that's making turbines and jet engines and diesel engines and a lot of heavy stuff—how does that bear on your life? Well, it bears on your life if you again leap over the immediate picture— a jet engine makes a plane fly, but a plane also has a big impact on your ability to get around and see your family. So the next step was to load this thing sideways with the other businesses that GE was involved in. I mean electricity impacts on you, power impacts on you, transportation impacts on you, consumer credit impacts on you. The issue was, how far can you go in this direction without hoking it up? That was the next stage and it yielded a slew of corporate commercials.

The objective was to draw the meaning of "We bring good things to life" to embrace the entire spectrum of innovative high technology products which GE provides to improve people's lives. The medical system's CAT scan, for example, was a brand new concept at that point and some of those commercials were done specifically to reinforce the innovative dimension and the caring dimension. The audience was an upscale portion of the total consuming population plus the important GE employees.

Gregory: Initially was there a great deal of in-fighting against this kind of expenditure? Did the product people say, "Hell, you're taking our money away from product advertising"?

Courtesy of General Electric.

White: No. At each stage along the line we were making presentations to the various divisions. Everybody intellectually understood. GE is a smart company, it has smart people and I think they knew there was a mess out there. Nobody was saying that they were doing a bad job, so the issue was how can we do this in a way that's going to work for the whole company and at the same time maintain the integrity of individual product programs? By creating something that's going to have greater impact market-wise than you can do by yourselves. Everybody said OK we hear you, the proof will be in the pudding.

Nobody was legislating what product advertising had to look like. They could work on their own product advertising as long as it appeared to have certain guidelines in terms of consumer benefit, and orientation as it related to the impact on their lives. They didn't have to win us over all the way through their advertising—they didn't. But what we did with each division was to create a feeling and a flavor for them that impacted on them, that featured their products but was also compatible with what we were doing.

So, in answer to your question, there was not overt resistance. There was skepticism, there was concern for turf, and there were a lot of frustrations in the on-going approval process, but I don't think there was an argument about the wisdom of the effort.

Gregory: Did you take it out to the plant communities?

White: Oh yes. Len Vickers [the head of consumer marketing at GE and previously at BBDO] was not only a driving force in the development stage as we were trying to make this thing come to life, he was also a driving force inside the company in terms of selling the concept, the need for this kind of an effort, right on down through the working units and ultimately conducting employee meetings.

Len Vickers presented in Churchillian tones (he's British, you know) an internal version of the presentation that we had made to Jack Welch. He made substantial changes and effectively made a presentation to their employees, which then took this advertising and related it to all the changes GE was making from signage to letterheads. It was an inspiring and major internal effort to make people realize how they were impacting on themselves as consumers and how important what they were doing was to the lives of the people around them. It was thrilling.

Gregory: Richard, how will you know when "We bring good things to life" has run its course? You've been doing it for ten years, when will it be time to change?

Costello: I don't know whether you know. I think if we had a fundamental change in the company. I can't imagine what that would be, but whatever it

Courtesy of General Electric.

Courtesy of General Electric.

was—if, for example, we stopped making good things—we'd have to stop. If it was found that it didn't fit our message, I think that would be the first key to a change. I think the second key driver of change is if quantative and qualitative research would find that we're running out of steam either in recall levels or whatever. Candidly I don't see that—the smartest thing is to stick to what you're doing, if it's working.

It's a well-liked campaign. People remember it. People like it. We seem to be able to manipulate it to create pretty much any story we want. So that's been its strength and we're not trying to change it anytime soon.

Gregory: Do you feel you have enough material to sustain it into the future?

Costello: We have this incredible company. I can take the best little stories all around, thrown them in as examples of bringing good things to life. We don't have to worry about consumer goods. If I've got a good story—go for it. I can go back in the company's history when I haven't got a good story today. For example, we lit the first baseball game, and link that with the fact that we light baseball stadiums today. This company is a huge enterprise with all this diversity—I don't have to sell just computers every day. I can dodge around and keep moving. That line can mean anything. Good things can be anything, saving a life, helping someone here, helping someone on the other side of the world, it doesn't really matter. It's a great line to work with, and it seems to be pretty effective. So I don't see it changing anytime soon.

XEROX—
"Putting It Together"

■ A conversation between the author and Michael Kirby, Director of Corporate Advertising and Promotion, Xerox Corporation.

———

Gregory: What does the new campaign theme "Putting It Together" stand for?

Kirby: The theme line "Putting It Together" means we put people together, we put equipment together, we put customers and prospects together, it's just endless. And it's emotionally driven, it has humanity.

Gregory: How does it work?

Kirby: What we have done is put together a series of strategic alliances with a lot of companies, some of them technical, some of them really business and sales oriented. So we've got ads waiting in the wings, to say "putting together Xerox and NYNEX," Xerox and Adobe, Xerox and Novelle, Interleaf, Intergraph, and so forth. It really makes the statement that we, as a company, are not trying to go it alone anymore. No one company can do it all. What we're beginning to realize is that if you establish strategic partners and combine the best of your resources with the best of other's resources, then you're providing document solutions to a lot of business problems.

Gregory: You are also repositioning the company as "The Document Company" in this campaign. What is behind this repositioning?

Kirby: Most executives don't think they have document problems. The irony is that based on the Gartener Group findings, the cost of documents and documentation is second only to payroll as an expense of doing business. We just take it for granted. We just do paperwork, whether it's electronic paperwork or hard copy paperwork, we just do it, and the costs associated with that are just staggering.

Gregory: What is the motivating factor to this repositioning?

Kirby: One of the things that is really frustrating for executive management is that they've got huge sum costs in technical investments. They're just not getting the productivity return they thought they were going to get out of it. A lot of it is because software is proprietary and there are proprietary operating systems, and when systems aren't connected, they aren't talking to each other. Until industry as a whole comes to grips with common standards, we're not going to get those yields. Therefore, we're not going to be able to convince any management team to invest higher and higher, as the products come down the pike. As a result, to first be competitive, we've got to provide a higher yield on productivity in human terms as well as business terms . . . it's really quite that simple. We think that this whole notion of repositioning Xerox as a document company is not only a good marketplace to be in, but it's a significant marketplace as well.

Gregory: Why did you change your positioning from "We Document the World" to the new one, "The Document Company"?

Kirby: "The Document Company" is a crisper articulation. The more we thought about how to dress it up, the more we were determined that it gave us a platform to say a lot more about the company. Documents are myriad, and they're used in a wide variety of ways, in business and industries. By being more focused, we saw more of a market.

Gregory: How did you determine the need to change that positioning? Was it because of the new products coming on line?

Kirby: Not really, although that was a consideration. The real need was to expand perceptions of our true capabilities—the name Xerox is synonymous with copying and while that's a huge asset, it also has limitations because we're just seen narrowly as a copier company, whereas we have enormous sales from electronic printing. We have workstations, Ethernet [the local area network], desktop publishing, faxing, typewriters, scanners, printers, and, of course, copiers. We're into so many businesses that touch and involve documents, that people aren't aware of, it became necessary to use this repositioning to expand people's perceptions of our capabilities.

Gregory: What do you consider the most challenging aspect of this campaign?

Kirby: The real challenge is to broaden perceptions and opportunities by talking about the document. And if you can get people to rethink the document in all of its manifestations, and associate yourself with those manifestations, then you've got a much better chance of them saying, "Aha, I see! So they [Xerox] are involved in all those other areas that get to providing document solutions to these business problems I've been worrying about." That's the opportunity and challenge as we saw it. Attack it from the product of our products, rather than the product themselves.

Gregory: Even the exhibit in your lobby makes one aware of the heritage of the document.

Kirby: Exactly, I mean we've always been in the document business, but because we invented modern copying, that fortunately has stayed with us, now we'd like to expand.

Gregory: What are the basic elements surrounding your new campaign?

Kirby: What we've done is use this whole "Putting It Together" theme, which comes from Stephen Sondheim's Broadway Show, called "Sunday in the Park with George," and the lead piece of music is "Putting It Together," and the whole lyrics of that song. It's as though Sondheim had written them to describe what we're doing here. We're in broadcast, both radio and television, which are wonderful tools to seed this whole document positioning.

Gregory: You launched the campaign in newspapers on two consecutive days. First with the "Putting It Together" spread announcement and followed up with the Docutech three full-page ads. Was that a planned roll out of the corporate campaign considering the second ad is a product ad?

Kirby: Yes. Absolutely by design, we had hoped to start earlier in order to give a foundation for the introduction of the Docutech series. As it was, we beat it by a day, but the *gestalt* of having fairly significant ads all in the *New York Times* and the *Wall Street Journal* on three consecutive days gave it sort of impact, and I think therefore it had as much meaning as if we'd started it two weeks earlier.

Gregory: When did you decide to use the music and lyrics from the Sondheim Broadway show?

Courtesy of Xerox Corporation.

Courtesy of Xerox Corporation.

Kirby: We embraced the whole "Putting It Together" theme along with the music and the lyrics about two weeks earlier, and it had run on radio. It is less obvious in print, and yet it's uniquely good in print, too, because it helps us express the many ways we put documents together, as well as our products, our salespeople with customers, our partnerships, etc.

Gregory: Do you plan to run primarily broadcast or will you continue with the print?

Kirby: The print effort is quite limited, but it's a function really of the budget this year, and the fact that the music and lyrics are important for the best effect.

Gregory: What about next year?

Kirby: This year we will primarily stay with radio and television. Starting next year, we'll come back in print because print is really a very strong market development medium. And by that, I mean, we'd like to talk to businesspeople in their medium, which invariably is print, and have them understand the importance of documents in their business life, the impact they have on the bottom line, and how they can do a better job with their documents. We've got some wonderful case histories where we present examples of using document solutions to solve business problems.

Gregory: How do you plan to measure the effectiveness of the campaign?

Kirby: We established a benchmark tracking study that we've done over time but there are three groups of key audiences that we go after and we do it through a third party research company. We will do two readings a year to monitor the progress of changing people's attitudes towards us.

Gregory: What are some of the questions you ask in your tracking studies?

Kirby: We may ask the question, "Can you name the company that manufactures or produces the following product?" and then we'll see if we've broadened people's perceptions. Or, we might say, "Can you name companies that concentrate on document solutions to business problems?" and we'll see whether that notion is getting through. Eventually, the study will get more pointed toward the advertising, so we can track communications value over time, and adjust messages if they're not working right or registering the desired result.

Gregory: How did you sell the repositioning internally?

Kirby: That's a very interesting question, and frankly, we're calling it employee marketing, which is a phrase of our Senior Vice President of Worldwide Monitoring, Len Vickers, because if you don't sell it internally, you won't sell it externally. We've got a lot of people in the field, such as direct salespeople and service technicians. If they don't understand why we have been re-positioned as "the document company" and what that means to our customers and our people, then they're not going to support it. They're not going to talk it up, and they're not going to be able to defend it. We asked Paul Allaire, our new CEO, if he would send a letter to every U.S. employee, and in fact, to every Xerox employee worldwide, in order to describe "The Document Company" and its meaning.

Gregory: We find that the support from senior management is absolutely essential in a corporate campaign. How did you generate support from your operating divisions?

Kirby: What I have done is form a worldwide communications council that convenes twice a year and has representation from all around the world to review communications issues. What I did for the new strategic repositioning campaign was to take two Europeans and two U.S. representatives and form a sub-group that gave the agency the briefing, who then came up with a campaign. This sub-group then sold it back into their communities. Once we were satisfied that from a functional standpoint, we were on to something, we presented it to the CEO and the senior management team.

Gregory: In a sense you had a worldwide consensus from the very beginning?

Kirby: That's right. You have to have a fundamental understanding of what you're trying to accomplish, both strategically and from a product standpoint, or from a solution standpoint. You've got to all work together, and if there's some central theme that helps drive them together in a seamless fashion, then you're ahead of the game. That's why this is an "idea" rather than an advertising execution. It is that theme that drives through everything, and not just advertising. It drives through our trade shows, our *Yellow Pages,* and our direct marketing. It drives through any form of communications channel that we want to use. So we are excited about it and think it has legs.

Gregory: You also changed agencies just recently. How did you manage it all?

Kirby: This has been a strange year. It seems like three years rolled into one. We gave five agencies the same briefing—all Xerox agencies so we didn't go on a fishing expedition.

Gregory: I know, we knocked on the door but nobody came.

Kirby: Oh God! My name is mud! [LAUGHTER] We really went into it by saying, we're not getting the exciting idea out of Backer, Spielvogel, Bates/NY, let's embrace other companies that have a deep knowledge of us from a business standpoint, who can crank up quickly, and let's give them all the same brief. What emerged was a very big idea from Y&R and it was head and shoulders above the rest of them. Not that we didn't get some good ideas, we did get some interesting executions, but we didn't get the big idea.

Gregory: It's the big idea that usually sells a campaign, isn't it?

Kirby: Exactly.

Gregory: When did you make the decision?

Kirby: July.

Gregory: Is that right? You turned this all around very quickly.

Kirby: Well, it's all the more so because we are very understaffed. I have two managers here. I think if we've got 40 people in this function in North America, we're lucky, and that's very lean.

Gregory: A lot has to be said for Y&R to be able to create it all so quickly.

Kirby: Yes. And Y&R's worked with us in Europe for a long time. And Joe De Deo, who was the European chairman, most recently was appointed worldwide chairman, so that was very useful because I've known Joe for many years, so he came in with an understanding of the company and where we wanted to go.

Gregory: What's the next aspect of the campaign?

Kirby: We have three commercials and they will rotate starting with the World Series through next December when we'll pull out for the holiday season. But, then we fully expect to go back in the new year with some market development advertising. The real iceberg is underneath the advertising, because you need promotion, public relations, a response center for inquiries, and you've also got to have an employee communications program. We need a training presentation that reinforces what "The Document Company" is about there. We've got a thousand-bed university down in Leesburg that's constantly being used for management and technical training. We've got trade shows that have to be constructed and conformed, all the collaterals worldwide, new products as they come up under "The Document Company," we've got event marketing, the Olympics, we've got Seville, the World's Fair. And so that's really what we're concentrating on right now. Putting together a comprehensive internal and external program that focuses on the document and utilizes the "Putting It Together" theme worldwide.

Gregory: Well, you've done a great job so far. I'm looking forward to seeing the rest of it.

Kirby: Yes, it's fun.

National CEO Survey: "Attitudes on Corporate Advertising"

■ While writing this book, we conducted a nationwide study of Chief Executive Officers of major corporations in order to gain further opinions and insights into the use of image advertising. A large cross-section of CEOs in a wide range of national companies were asked to participate.

All respondents had many things of interest to say about the value and use of image advertising—some of which have been incorporated in the main text of this book. Here are a few additional thoughts from the CEOs on brand image advertising that we thought would be of value to you.

"Corporate image advertising affords a way to communicate effectively to customers, potential customers, employees, and opinion leaders the character of our company . . . in a disciplined and cost-effective manner. . . . It's an important part of our total program to build awareness of the ICI brand and act as an umbrella over our diverse product advertising." ICI Americas Inc.

"In the financial service business, the brand image is the leverage point in any transaction." Merrill Lynch & Co. Inc.

"We wouldn't be doing it [image advertising] if we did not feel it was paying its own way. . . ." The Dow Chemical Company

"It's an increasingly important element in our marketing arsenal." Citgo Petroleum Corporation

"Corporate ads enable us to communicate with key audiences on critical issues." Brown & Williamson Tobacco

"It [corporate image advertising] is valuable in establishing brand awareness covering a wide mix of products and services . . . adds value to the marketing process because it eliminates the need for sales people to waste (time) in establishing company credentials . . . makes it easier to introduce new products." Contel Corporation

"Corporate image advertising helps build the level of company name recognition and creates a positive perception of our products and services. In addition, it helps offset unfavorable publicity and negative attitudes." Aetna

"[Corporate image advertising] strengthens company's position as a reliable supplier of gas. As a credible source of information (it) serves us well during times of change or when community support is needed." ONG

"We feel it's extremely important [to build] public image, attract good employees, [encourage] pride in present employees, reinforce present and attract new customers." Spartan Stores Inc.

"[Image advertising] is an excellent long term investment in building a strong image for the corporation and creating an umbrella for the company's divisions and products." Figgie International Inc.

"It is very important to put on a 'good face' to our public. As a regulated utility, we depend upon goodwill from our customers. . . . [Image advertising] is very important in our external programs." Georgia Power Company

"It [image advertising] creates a positive environment for selling: predisposes customers and prospects toward our institution; reinforces customers' decision to bank with us; differentiates us from other institutions; creates increased recognition and awareness of our name; boosts employee spirits." Citizens and Southern Corp.

"Trust, integrity and stewardship are important concepts in our business and are best communicated via image advertising." Massachusetts Mutual Life Insurance Co.

"[Image advertising is] highly important on a global scale." E I Du Pont de Nemours Co.

"Targeted corporate advertising helps create a positive environment for our sales and service efforts." Lincoln National Corporation

"We want to communicate to our key constituents the nature of our core businesses and the overall personality of the company. Corporate advertising is the best means of doing this on a mass scale." GTE Corporation

"Establishing a clear and differentiated image is critical to our future. Corporate advertising has successfully managed our company through a significant name change and a new positioning for key audiences, both internally and externally." H N Bull Information Systems

Corporate Identification Checklist

■ This does not purport to be an exhaustive list of all possible materials to carry your corporate name. You can surely add others. But it is a good starting point for those faced with the task of changing a corporate identity.

1. Stationery

   a. Letterhead, general

   b. Letterhead, executive

   c. Business card, general

   d. Business card, executive

   e. Envelope, #10

   f. Envelope, executive

   g. Envelope, window

     h. Statement

     i. Purchase form

     j. Office memo

     k. Acknowledgment

     l. Shipping papers

     m. News release

     n. Name, phone, address change mailer

2. Literature

     a. Annual report

     b. Quarterly report

     c. Capabilities and services brochure

     d. Catalog binder

     e. Catalog pages

     f. Replacement pages

     g. Public relations information

     h. Sales bulletin

     i. "Literature You Requested"

     j. Newsletter

     k. Corporate identity manual

     l. Specification sheets

     m. External house organ

3. Transportation

     a. Truck cab

     b. Pick-up van

     c. Trailer body

     d. Parking lot decal

     e. Business car

     f. Company aircraft

     g. Ship

     h. Freight and tank car

    i. Materials-handling equipment

    j. Bumper stickers

4. Packing

    a. Folding carton

    b. Label

    c. Flexible packing (bags, sheets, wraps)

    d. Paper bag

    e. Wrapping paper

    f. Plastic container

    g. Plastic bags

    h. Glass containers

    i. Can

    j. Tube

    k. Rigid containers

    l. Closure

    m. Hang tag

    n. Cloth label

    o. Gift box

    p. Product identification (nameplate)

    q. Shipping containers (crate, corrugated box)

    r. Tape

    s. Decal

    t. Stencil

    u. Stamp

5. Architecture

    a. Exterior design

    b. Interior design

    c. Interior lobby

    d. Interior entrance

    e. Office, showroom, store furnishings, and fixture decor

    f. Landscaping

6. Signs

   a. Exterior (fascia, pylon)

   b. Interior

   c. Directional

   d. Directory

   e. Decals

   f. Remote

7. Marketing/Sales

   a. Sales manual

   b. Uniform

   c. Lapel pin

   d. Audio-visual

   e. Portable exhibits and displays

   f. Permanent exhibits and displays

   g. Radio scripts

   h. Newspaper advertisements

   i. Television advertisements

   j. Magazines, consumer

   k. Magazines, trade and business

   l. Booklets and brochures

   m. Direct mail

   n. Posters

   o. Outdoor boards

   p. Yellow Pages advertising

   q. Shopping carts

   r. Logo sheets

   s. Co-op materials

   t. Window displays

   u. Merchandising aids

   v. Giveaways

Index